"In my personal opinion as a career sales leader, *Engage Me* captures a masterful framework for building a high performance sales organization. It is clear from Kevin's experience, examples and models that high performance does not come from one secret ingredient but from a multi-faceted combination of interdependent concepts that must be consistently and deliberately lived by leaders.

I was particularly struck by the careful balance between business growth and people growth – which cannot be dissociated. This balance requires clarity of expectations, both what and how, and the managerial courage to set up and maintain positive performance tension.

If you're in the market to deliver results through a sales team committed to great performance, *Engage Me* is a must read!"

— Paul Lirette, President, GlaxoSmithKline Inc.

"The great leaders I admire most are those who can both envision on a grand scale but, if necessary, execute down to the finest detail. Kevin Higgins is one of those leaders and he shares both in this book."

— Greig Clark, Founder of College Pro Painters

"As a sales professional and sales leader, I've seen firsthand the impact of these tools across sales organizations. *Engage Me* works. Buy it. Use it."

— Craig Wortmann, CEO, Sales Engine Inc., Clinical Professor of Entrepreneurship, University of Chicago's Booth School of Business, Author of *What's Your Story?*

"Fusion has embedded these disciplines within my sales organization. Higgins provides the essential ingredients to help Sales Leaders turn common sense into common practice."

— Lou Gizzarrelli, President, Neopost Canada

"Higgins shares sales management strategies that are practical with broader application beyond the sales force."

— Bill Maurin, Acting CEO, Meridian

ENGAGE ME

STRATEGIES FROM THE
SALES EFFECTIVENESS SOURCE

KEVIN HIGGINS

fusion!
LEARNING INC.

For information about special discounts for bulk purchases, or to book Kevin Higgins to speak at your live event, please contact Fusion Learning at 416-424-2999, or visit our website at *www.fusionlearninginc.com*.

ISBN: 978-0-9920771-0-5

Fusion Learning Inc.
272 Richmond Street East, Suite 200,
Toronto, Ontario M5A 1P4

Publishing Consultant:
Brilliant Idea Books

Editing:
Catherine Leek of Green Onion Publishing

Interior Design and Formatting:
Kim Monteforte of WeMakeBooks.ca

Cover Design:
Kim Monteforte of WeMakeBooks.ca

Printed in Canada

Foreword

July 9, 2008, I remember the day like it was yesterday. I was at my first Fusion Learning Strategic Blue*PRINT* Offsite. It was held at founder Tim Magwood's cottage.

It was the first time I came face to face with the incredible Fusion Learning Culture. The culture at Fusion Learning can be summarized in a few key phrases, "Work hard, play hard, results matter, but having fun is key." I was there as the new chair of their Advisory Board. The partners of the business were far-sighted enough to know that they didn't know everything and an Advisory Board could help them face strategic issues and solve problems better.

The goal of the 2-day offsite was simple — have fun *and* turn out a Strategic *BluePRINT* (SB) for the business for the next 3 years. The Fusion Learning SB is an amazing piece of paper. In just one page it summarizes the keys for the business for the next 3 years. It is one of the best focusing documents I have ever seen and, in business, focus is king. Proctor and Gamble was famous for getting their business plan down to four pages; Fusion Learning has it down to one. It hangs on every person's wall at Fusion. It hangs on mine. More important … *it works.*

On that warm July day I participated in a number of small groups and took the opportunity to get to know a number of the team members and learn more about this amazing company. As is my habit, I always try to discover what makes a company tick. I love Peter Drucker's three questions.

1. What Business are you in?
2. Who are your customers?
3. Why do they buy from you?

I find the wide variety of answers I get to these questions from different people within the same company fascinating. This day it was pretty clear.

The answers to the first two questions were usually some version of, "We are in the Sales Effectiveness Training Business" and "We sell to big companies with sales forces." It was the answers to the third question where the lights really flashed. Over and over people from program designers to facilitators to executives would repeat, one on one or in groups, "They buy from us because our stuff really works!" When I probed them on how they knew this, they would elaborate with great pride some examples they were personally involved with. "If it doesn't work and really change behavior and results, we don't want to do it," one person told me.

Later in the big group session we were working on what I call the "top box" of the SB — what positioning we wanted to have; what we stood for. When it was my turn to speak, I asked Tim, who was facilitating, if I could digress and tell a little story. Being the consummate story teller himself, he said, "Sure. Fill your boots."

I told them about the time I was in New York City, the week after I had graduated from Ivey Business School at the University of Western Ontario. I was out on the town, in the heart of capitalism, dreaming about conquering Wall Street. I remember distinctly walking along the southern side of Central Park, taking it all in. Just ahead of me was a young teenager carrying a boom box on his shoulder, listening to the music. Just as we approached a couple of police cruisers, parked just 3 feet away from us, one of them, for no apparent reason, let its siren blare. The car didn't move. It just sat there with its siren blasting away. I turned to look, but the boy in front of me didn't bother. He just kept walking straight ahead. Out of the side of his mouth he said, "I'm glad it woiks, fellas. I'm glad it woiks."

I loved that line and it was my suggested tagline for Fusion. "It Woiks!"

And it does. Over the last 7 years I have seen countless examples of Fusion Learning help companies develop solid, effective sales management practices that really "woik" and produce fantastic results. Kevin will tell you many of these stories in *Engage Me*, but more importantly he'll tell you *why* they work and *how* to get them for yourself.

Which brings me to author, Kevin Higgins. I have known Kevin for 28 years, since he was a franchise manager for me at College Pro Painters in 1985 and 1986. He was a top performer there. He was a top performer at Forum. He is a top notch CEO at Fusion. The CEOs I have always admired most are those who can both envision on a grand scale and, yet, if necessary, execute down to the finest detail. Kevin is one of those CEOs, and he shares both skills with you in this amazing book.

Kevin's middle initial should be "D" for *Discipline*. It is core to everything he does and it is built into the selling model for Fusion Learning. Vince Lombardi used to say,

"Practice doesn't make perfect. Perfect practice makes perfect."

Perfect sales management practices are laid out for you in *Engage Me.*

Enjoy it. I did.

Greig Clark
Founder of College Pro Painters
July 2013

Contents

PART III   SALES MANAGEMENT DISCIPLINES

Great Sales Culture = Engaged Sales Team

This book is not theoretical. It is a practical guide with the attitude, skills and disciplines you need to possess for an engaged sales force that will deliver above-plan performance. A lot of what you will read is common sense; it is not always common practice.

Many of us are familiar with the research that says people don't leave companies, they leave managers. We agree! The "we" refers to myself and my colleagues at Fusion Learning. Fusion Learning is a sales performance firm. Our vision is to be "The Sales Effectiveness Source." The content of this book has been developed over the last 10 years as we have worked with hundreds of clients and thousands of sales leaders to help them dramatically improve their sales organizations.

Here's just a little of the feedback we've received over the years.

- "We came in at 140% of plan. Some might say 'Well, maybe your plan was wrong.' No, it was our most aggressive plan in years." Wade Stayzer, Vice President, Retail, Meridian Credit Union

- "We needed to change from a transaction-driven service culture to a proactive sales culture. The process has produced impressive results, freeing up significant time for Account Managers to meet with clients and improve sales productivity. To date, the initiative has delivered net profit of $487,798." Jacinthe Higgins, Director of Learning Strategies, Business Development Bank of Canada

- "We saw double-digit sales growth in a flat market, and had the Top Hewitt engagement scores within Neopost globally among 15 countries." Lou Gizzarelli, President, Neopost Canada

- "The results far exceeded our expectations ... insurance enrolment more than doubled; balance transfers increased by 89%; account retention increased by 50% ... sustainable results that will pay out for many years to come." Scott Williams, former AVP, Customer Contact Centre, Canadian Tire Financial Services

- "Our dozen strategic brands grew at 3 times industry growth. That's a key indicator for the success of our work with Fusion." Rick Tousaw, Vice President, Ontario, Molson Coors

- "I've experienced a lot of sales training initiatives over the years ... at Hewlett-Packard, at BMO ... and the Fusion session was the best 2-day experience I've had in my career ... it wasn't necessarily *what* was taught; it was *how* the program was delivered." Megan Kells, Managing Director & Head of Canadian Sales & Client Service, Global Treasury Management, BMO Capital Markets

The numbers are impressive — the "how" is engagement.

People leave managers — but why? They are not being coached, developed, motivated to be their best. They choose a "greener pasture." With that premise, we will review the attitude, skills and key sales management disciplines that, when practiced consistently, will continually coach, develop and motivate your sales team. They will be engaged and will not look for greener pastures.

The title, *Engage Me*, is the outcome we must achieve — a sales force that is productive and engaged. The cycle of poor engagement is a frequent occurrence in organizations. A survey is conducted. The organization is unhappy with its engagement scores. They also have higher personnel turnover than they would like to see. The senior leadership team meets and forms a committee to study the issue. They get lots of information and a plan is formulated. The plan involves many tactics but often missing is that managers' need to be much better at managing. If managers are great at managing and leading, their people will be engaged and they will not leave.

In implementing the ideas in *Engage Me*, I encourage you to adopt a "progress not perfection" mentality. Look for small changes that deliver strong results. Do not attempt to implement everything at once. Read the book in full and then decide on one area of sales management to change. Work on that change until it is a habit and then move to your next change.

Our clients often adopt our sales management disciplines and then take them beyond the sales team. You will see that most of what we discuss, from coaching to feedback to one-on-ones to performance reviews, can apply beyond the sales organization so feel free to share the book and the ideas with your colleagues outside the sales organization.

My team at Fusion Learning (www.fusionlearninginc. com) is always ready to help your sales organization with its sales culture. We believe a great sales culture has three components (see graphical representation of a great sales culture).

1. Sales Strategy
2. Sales Management Disciplines
3. Sales Process

SALES CULTURE

© 2014 Fusion Learning Inc.

This book addresses the second of these three components. The sales management disciplines required to have a great sales culture and an engaged sales team are:

- Consistent and focused sales coaching and feedback.
- Monthly One-on-Ones that are strategic and tactical as well as business and salesperson focused.
- Weekly or bi-weekly sales meetings that build skill and motivation.
- Frequent Field Coaching with manager as coach and cheerleader, not as captain.
- Bi-weekly pipeline management that focuses on overall pipeline health as well as individual deals.

Engage Me will provide a clear process and best practices for each of these disciplines.

This book is intended for all Sales Leaders in all types of businesses. With no sales, there is no company. So if you are a business leader, this book will give you concrete how-tos to dramatically increase the success of your sales organization as demonstrated in the results shared by our clients. The book is not a substitute for training; it is a kick-start before training or a great source book after training.

I wrote this book as a business leader, as a coach, as a trainer and as a salesperson. I will at times switch "voices" depending on the chapter and the content. Please enjoy the different styles and when we meet I will just be me.

Properly executing the learning in *Engage Me* will lead to a productive and engaged sales team. Enjoy!

PART I

ATTITUDE

The attitude required to *Engage Me* (where Me is your sales team) is one of a high performing team. "We win together and I win individually." The one chapter in this section deals with sales culture. The definition I find most useful of culture is "the way we do things around here." It is not something that is written; it is how things are done.

I will talk about the Fusion Learning culture, not because it is perfect but because it is a strong example of culture and it delivers results — a compound annual growth rate of 28% over the last 10 years. Please do not try to copy it. Take what is great in your culture and add in some new, fresh ideas that you pick up here.

This chapter will introduce you to results from Fusion Learning's Sales Culture Survey. The survey has three main components, matching the three components of a great sales culture outlined in the introduction.

1. Sales Strategy
2. Sales Management Disciplines
3. Sales Process

The Fusion Learning Sales Culture Survey will be quoted at the start of each chapter. It was conducted in 2006, 2010 and in 2013. The respondents were from multiple industries.

- Financial services
- High technology/Office products
- Telecommunications
- Professional services
- Pharmaceutical
- Software
- Media/Entertainment
- Packaged goods

The respondents had sales forces that ranged from 50 to 500+ and revenues ranged from less than $100 million (18%) to $100 million-$1 billion (45%) to over $1 billion (37%). Many questions were repeated on all three Fusion Learning Sales Culture Surveys but not all. In the 2013 survey we added a number of new questions and dropped some that we had found not as useful. The data reflects a generic viewpoint. Use it as a reference point for your organization and how you stack up against peers in the same and different industries.

Engage Me is about having a great sales culture. Let's begin with that.

Sales Culture

THE RESEARCH

The Question: "We currently have a high performing sales culture."

The Response 2013: 6.1 on a 10-point scale (where 1 is not at all and 10 is most definitely); 58% of respondents replied with 6 out of 10 or lower.

STRENGTHS

- Strong sales cultures are easy to spot — they consistently deliver above-plan performance.
- 22% of organizations ranked themselves between 8 and 10. They have a strong culture and they know it.

OPPORTUNITY

- Weak sales cultures rely on heroics — a few strong performers are driven to make the numbers.
- Consistency is not present.
- Senior management lives in fear of the bad month, quarter, or year.

DEFINITION

- A process with the right attitude, skills and disciplines for salespeople and sales leaders that holds salespeople accountable for delivering above-plan performance in a way that supports our values and our culture.
- Sales Culture that is metrics driven and predictable.

FUSION LEARNING POINT OF VIEW

- Sales Culture is a complex web — a mesh of structure, process, reward, recognition, compensation, training, leading, motivating, coaching, teaching, providing feed-back, etc.

GOAL

A sales culture that delivers consistent above-plan perfor-mance quarterly and annually.

Everyone can have a bad month, just don't have three in a row!

PERSONAL EXPERIENCE — COMPOUND GROWTH

Fusion Learning has been a Profit 200 company in Canada[1] for 7 consecutive years, with a compound annual growth rate of 28%. Everything you read in this book is practiced by our sales force. Follow this formula and you will have a strong sales culture. We did not design the culture; it was more of an evolution.

In 2002, Fusion Learning was me and Tim Magwood, the founder of Fusion. We were not at all disciplined; we were two individuals trying to create a company. A key turning point was early in 2008 when, after 7 years of consistent growth, we woke up one day and said, "We are in trouble, we have very little booked business and an extremely thin pipeline."

We began what became known as our "all hands on deck" period and formalized many informal disciplines (especially sales meetings and pipeline reviews) and moved from a sales team based on individual performance to a very solid team-based approach. We also took prospecting from an individual sport to a team sport.

What you will read is the culmination of our experience and the experience of the clients we have helped in a journey toward a strong sales culture that delivers results (see Great Sales Culture = Engaged Sales Team). Many sales organizations have the components discussed in this book but may not have the results — look at the "quality" within your disciplines, if you feel the quantity is there but results are not. This is not meant as "the" formula, this is meant as the formula that works for Fusion Learning. Use what you feel fits for your sales organization.

---

[1] The top 200 fastest growing companies in Canada as named by *Profit* magazine.

Creating Your Sales Culture

Every organization has its own environment. Like the basic company values, the culture within the sales department will reflect some of the organization's features. However, every sales culture within an enterprise has definite and specific needs. These requirements are common across all sales cultures, no matter the industry or organization. In our 2013 Fusion Learning Sales Culture Survey we asked a new question: "We are happy with the current state of our sales culture." The response was 5.4 on a 10-point scale. Ouch! Seventy percent of respondents rated their happiness with the culture as 6 out of 10 or lower. The need for improvements in sales culture is clear. Where is your organization? What will you do to ensure you can say, "I am happy with our sales culture *and* with our sales performance."

Creating and encouraging a strong sales culture is a mesh of elements and attitudes. Every chapter in this book will help you to develop a strong sales culture. Let's get started with the "attitude" components.

- Company Values
- Fusion Learning Culture A to Z
- Coaching Mind-Set
- Company Meeting Structure

Company Values

A company's values will vary across industries, with company leaders and as the values within a society change and develop. Some organizations will explicity define the values they and their employees aspire to while others will not; but make no mistake that the values exist. An organization's values reflect the way they interact with customers, suppliers and employees.

At Fusion Learning we have five company values.

1. Communicate & Collaborate
2. Lead Creatively
3. Learn & Grow
4. Deliver Excellence
5. Celebrate & Appreciate

These are not just a poster on our wall. We live and breathe these every day. Those who exemplify them are rewarded and those who break the values consistently will not be with our team for long. They are not words; they are a code of conduct. They help our sales team to have a great culture. Let's talk about ways we keep them alive and part of daily life at Fusion Learning.

1. We have a values board in our office and when a team member sees someone demonstrating a value they write the value on a post-it note and provide a brief description of who and how the value was demonstrated. They post it on the board (actually using a tack as the post-it glue wears out). We have weekly and monthly meetings where we take time to ask team members to add to the board.

2. When the values board gets full we pull them and organize them into bundles for each person. At our monthly team meeting we share the notes in different fun ways: pick your best; share two with a partner; read them and then thank a few people who nomi-

nated you; summarize a theme from your nominations; share a value you were not recognized for and what you will do to be nominated next month for it.

3. We recognize the nominations with fun awards. One time it was candy for each nomination. Another time nominees picked a prize from a selection, with those with most nominations going first. At one especially fun meeting we had 50 nominations and we gave cash prizes from $1 to $50. Every person nominated had one paper with their name in a hat. The first 20 names pulled got $1 each. The second 20 names pulled got $2 each. The next 5 names got $5. The next 4 names got $10. The final name pulled got $50. It cost $175 but was a thrilling competition and it was abundantly clear that our values matter and we are willing to pay those who demonstrate them.

4. Performance reviews (read more in Chapter Nine) have two main sections — strengths and opportunities. Within these two main sections 80% of feedback collected is organized by our five values. What people do well lines up with them and where they need to improve is organized by the values. (A very interesting side note is that the category most consistently with a low number of comments is Celebrate & Appreciate. We do a lot to celebrate and appreciate as you will hear throughout this chapter — yet it is not enough as shown by the low number of comments in performance reviews. I mention this here as it is imperative to have a healthy, healthy injection of celebrate and appreciate in order to have a great sales culture.)

5. Our annual Shareholders Award is given to those who demonstrate, not some, but all of our values on a consistent basis during the year. It is an employee-nominated award and to submit a colleague you must give one example of each value that you saw them demonstrate during the year.

6. Management discusses team members and they are frequently reviewed against the Fusion Learning Values.

7. Every team member has a framed copy of the values on their desk.

8. We have a Values Conference Room, which has a huge poster of our Values (new addition to our most recent office expansion).

9. New hires are evaluated on how well we feel they will live our values — they must have convinced us that they will be able to consistently demonstrate or they will not be hired. Most critical is Learn and Grow, which we test for in our simulation process.

10. When we lose a team member, we conduct exit interviews and we often see issues where they did not demonstrate our values.

Values are the first component of a great sales culture. Be careful that they are lived, not *just* a poster on the wall. Have the team help to create them and be sure that you, as a sales leader, demonstrate them consistently. This definitely leads to a to-do — create them or revisit them. Is your organization Values Driven?

Fusion Learning Culture A to Z

One of our goals at Fusion Learning is to be recognized as a top employer. We have not yet won that honor, but I know we will. We are going above and beyond in creating a great atmosphere at Fusion Learning with highly engaged people. What keeps me awake at night is, "What are we missing? What else should we be doing?"

Recently, on a day that this was bothering me (truth be told, another list of top employers came out, one that we were too small to apply for, and as I reviewed the facts provided for what made them the cream of the crop, it felt like we had it all and then some), I created the A to Z of culture at Fusion Learning. Actually, I got to 17 of 26 and then I went to our kitchen for Beer Fridays and had our team help me complete it.

Here is the list, with explanations. I am not suggesting that you need to follow this list to have a great sales culture; I provide it as a list of examples that can help you create your A to Z culture list. Undoubtedly you will notice how Fusion Learning's attitude — its values and coaching mindset — work into this list.

A. **Annual Incentive Trip** — If the team passes its annual stretch target (usually about 15% over budget), they are rewarded with an incentive trip. Past years have included Cancun, Jamaica, New York City and Collingwood.

B. **Birthdays** — Birthdays are celebrated with cake, candles and singing. You even get your choice of cake!

C. **Club Membership** — All employees get up to $80 per month to pay for a health club membership or a fitness activity.

D. **December Holiday Party** — Not to be missed — drinks, gourmet meals and live entertainment.

E. **Employee Onboard Plan** — Our New Hire Onboarding Plan helps transition all new employees. We believe it to be best in class (more on that in Chapter Four).

F. **Food** — Grocery Gateway delivers every week to stock fresh fruit, bagels, granola bars, yogurt and healthy snacks (no junk food allowed).

G. **Gong** — With every new deal the salesperson bangs the gong to celebrate the new client and share with the team how we won.

H. **Halloween Party** — No average Halloween party! The team dresses up and acts like one other member.

I. **Initiation** — Rapid fire on day one with all team members asking a personal question.

J. **Juice, Coffee and Pop** — All free, all the time (with request for your favorite flavors).

K. **Knowledge Enhancement** — Training, development and special interest courses, including French, Spanish, Accounting and Photography.

L. **Liquor Fridays** — Company sponsored team beer/snacks every Friday (Thursdays in the summer).

M. **Monthly Updates** — Open-book management to share exactly how we are doing, including revenues and profitability.

N. **No Butts Deal** — Smokers are encouraged to quit by having no butts for one year and the company pays for a one-week Caribbean vacation — three successful graduates so far ...

O. One-on-Ones — Every employee has a formal One-on-One with their manager monthly. These are in-depth reviews that recognize success and help to build skill (see Chapter Five).

P. Play Space — A recent office renovation included an 800-square-foot play space, including ping-pong, darts and HD TV.

Q. Quarterly Bonus — Every employee at Fusion Learning has received a quarterly bonus every quarter for 10 years.

R. Retirement Savings — The company matches up to $3500 annually.

S. Summer Retreat — Three-day off-site retreat every year to build skills and the team — locations have included Muskoka, Haliburton and Niagara-on-the-Lake.

T. Taxi and Dinner — Stay past 7 pm and they are paid for.

U. Unique Work Space — Brick, beams, open concept and glass.

V. Vacation — 3 weeks to start plus 6 personal days; 4 weeks at 4 years and 5 weeks after 7 years.

W. Wheel to Win — For every new deal, a salesperson chooses a co-worker who helped them get the deal. The co-worker spins a wheel for a gift card valued from $5 to $50.

X. eXternal Fun Days — Once per quarter a fun day — past days include bowling, sailing, patio drinks, team competition, charity visits.

Y. Yoga — Weekly yoga session in the play space.

Z. **Zoo Days** — Bring your pet to the office — Kipling, Kya and Ellie have joined us so far.

Coaching Mind-Set

Great sales cultures view the sales team as a learning organization that can always improve. Exceptional sales managers convey this attitude by looking for opportunities to groom and prime salespeople in the company's values. Coaching should be a chief activity.

I BELIEVE!

A story from my former CEO that helps to illustrate this principle.

Our industry had created a productivity norm for salespeople that the average salesperson could sell $1 million in training per year. Everybody knew the norm and if they had 10 salespeople they expected $10 million in revenue. Twenty salespeople meant $20 million. During a management meeting, our CEO jumped on his soapbox and proclaimed, "Why can't the average be $2 million per salesperson? We have people who sell that amount, so it is possible. And if we get the average to $2 million, we will probably have someone selling $3 or $4 million."

At the time we had just over 30 salespeople and just over $30 million in revenue. Fast forward a few years and the results — just over 30 salespeople and just over $60 million in revenue. With one salesperson breaking the $5-million mark! How did we do it? A strong sales culture with a clear goal to improve.

The sales organizations that do not believe their own press always look to improve. Sales managers are the heart and soul of this consistent improvement. They constantly look to:

- **Develop Sales Team Capabilities:** Every performer can improve from new to veteran, from below plan to above plan. The manager and the sales leadership team must constantly be looking for ways to take their game to the next level. What are we doing to break the mold, change the game and stay ahead of the competition?

- **Build Relationships with Salespeople:** Each salesperson is unique. Each salesperson needs a strong manager. They need help, support, guidance and often a swift kick in the butt.

- **Create Value in All Coaching:** Each coaching moment — a One-on-One, a funnel review, field coaching and fly-bys must add value to the salesperson. They must say that was a good use of my time. I am better off for spending time with my manager.

These principles are not rocket science but they must be present to create a great sales culture. Are you modeling these in your sales organization?

Company Meeting Structure

Another huge part of culture is team gatherings. These can range from casual to formal from team to organization; they can be used to celebrate and reward or inform and set challenges. The best sales cultures have a structure that keeps people connected to the business and driving to surpass the stated goals. Meetings set the tone for your culture. (Chapter Six will discuss sales team meetings in more detail.) The ideas in the chapter can apply to any meeting.

BREAKFAST INCLUDED

My first sales role was at Xerox. Without dating myself, they were, at the time, known as the best sales culture. They had meetings down pat. Every Monday morning at 8 am, every salesperson was in a meeting room with their team and their manager to kick start the sales week.

It worked. We were there. We got the week started early. They also held monthly district meetings. All five sales teams gathered to hear the update versus the plan, celebrate some success and share some war stories. Prospecting Blitz Days were held about once a month. Then there were the informal meetings. Lunch with anywhere from three to eight colleagues at Swiss Chalet once a week.

When our district manager became a stickler for in the office at 8 am and on the road by 9 am, it was not odd to find the need for a hearty breakfast with colleagues at a local diner just after 9 am — if he only knew where he had driven us! These meetings — formal and informal — were a huge part of the great Xerox sales culture that I fondly remember.

Company meetings take some planning and tend to be of a more formal nature. Here are some ideas and guidelines for frequency.

- **Sales Team Meetings:** Weekly! My belief is sales is an hourly, daily, weekly activity and even the most sophisticated sales force with incredibly long sales cycles can benefit from interaction with colleagues and management. This assumes an interactive, productive meeting that delivers value to participants.

- **Division/Company Updates:** Monthly! From 20 to 200 to 2000 people, with modern technology, it is possible. Live, conference call, webinar and e-mail with an embedded video from the leader can reach the desired group. Keep your team informed. Thank them for their service. Reward and recognize the above and beyond effort. Information leads to connection and connection leads to engagement.

- **Training Sessions:** Daily! Just kidding. I am in the training business so I need to put in a plug when I can. Seriously, every salesperson should get 5 days of training annually — 2 should be product/service and 3 days should be skills training.

- **Off-sites:** Semi-annually! Two critical elements to off-sites — formal and informal. What happens at the bar at midnight is often as important as what happens during the address from the CEO. Both are important. Semi-annual is fine, as one can be a smaller, local gathering, maybe just the sales team and one can be larger — a regional, national or international meeting to build skill, motivation, connection and society.

- **Holiday Parties:** Annually! Hold it in January if the December prices are too high. Organizations who put on an event for their team get great publicity with spouses, friends, family and all who will listen to what a great party the company threw! Those who have adopted austerity measures get five times more bad press for being skimpy, cheap and, as often heard in the corridors, "not caring about their people." Fusion Learning throws a huge holiday party every year. You will read the good, the bad and the ugly later in the book and it says, "The annual holiday party is not to be missed." We go over the top in venue, food, music and libations and it usually costs us 10 basis points — a 10th of 1% of our annual revenues.

This list applies to company meetings, not included are many department and internal meetings that are also critical.

Off-site meetings are a very important cultural building tool when done right. You'll find some great tips for holding off-site meetings in Figure 1.

A strong sales culture is a process that has the right attitude, skills and disciplines for salespeople and sales leaders. It is metrics driven and predictable. We have begun the journey with some ideas on Values, including Fusion Learning's Culture List, Mind-Set, and Meeting Structure. With a robust attitude in place, sales managers need to develop skills to convey these ideas to their teams. Attitude is the first building block to creating an engaged and winning sales culture!

Figure 1: **Top 10 Conference Tips**

1. **Do nothing until you answer this question: "What do I want to see my people do differently as a result of the conference?"** By creating Outcome-Focused Activity rather than Agenda-Focused Schedules, you will be a leader of change, setting more actionable tasks for your team to grab hold of and run with.

2. **Include an "Open Mic" or "Questions and Answers" time hosted by executives.** By merging management members in the learning session with your team, you'll ensure corporate goals and daily activities mesh, thus increasing opportunities for individual success as part of the corporate mandate.

3. **Invite Clients to the meeting, and create structured learning activities with them.** Their feedback will be instructive, ensuring authentic scenarios lead to real world success strategies.

4. **Frequently put people in teams or groups to demonstrate the most recent learning and skills, i.e., Mid-Morning Recall Game.** You'll ensure participants are consistently paying keen attention, "learning by doing." Repetition is essential!

5. **Encourage executive presentations to have less detail and more activities.** The process of learning works best when participants focus on doing a few things really well, rather than trying to do many things sparsely.

6. **Include "White Space" — allow times for people to have unscheduled downtime.** Sure, intense "boot camps" sound like you mean business; but employees who sense that the company cares about them as people by offering them a quality experience will always give back more.

7. **Cross-pollination — have time in regions, AND have learning activities for people across regions to share challenges, successes, etc.** This isn't just a head office meeting! It's important for everyone to feel fully involved on a highly personal level.

8. **Invest in the sizzle (location, entertainment, award dinners, etc.) as well as the steak (workshop design and content).** A prudent blend of education and relaxation always makes for more memorable and impactful learning, while rewarding success.

9. **Remember that workshops can have:**
   - Presentations
   - Multi-media
   - Stations
   - Role plays/real plays
   - Pairs, trios, teams
   - Competitive exercises
   - Simulations
   - Games
   - Debates

10. **Think of at least one activity each day that can remove people from their comfort zone.** This will help them think outside the box, promoting self-examination of their skills, attitudes and the views that they are accustomed to following ... all of which leads to discovering ways to make improvements in their daily approach to their work.

© 2014 Fusion Learning Inc.

PART II

SKILLS

We have the right attitude to create a great sales culture and we are going to look at the sales management disciplines required, but before we do, we must visit the fundamentals of great sales management — coaching and feedback.

Think of your favorite sport — they all have fundamentals that require constant focus and constant work to continuously "sharpen the saw." Golf has grip, stance and swing. Tennis has grip, forehand, backhand and serve. Even the most accomplished professionals who have won many tournaments spend more time practicing the fundamentals than they spend playing matches.

Coaching and feedback, when done correctly and frequently, will elicit engagement. If your salespeople are constantly improving, how can they not be engaged? One professional services firm used to publicize to new hires that they were not the highest paying firm but they were the best at coaching. Those who joined them would learn faster and climb the ranks quicker, ultimately leading them to make more money than if they went to a higher paying competitor.

The two chapters in this section will not "teach" coaching and feedback but rather encourage you to hold up a mirror to your skills. You have what it takes to be excellent at coaching and feedback, no additional skills are needed. You do need to examine how you are using the skills to ensure you are effective so that you create a great sales culture that delivers strong business results and an engaged sales team.

Question Better, Confirm More, Respond Less

THE RESEARCH

The Question: "We have a strong culture of coaching, development, and continuous improvement in our sales organization."

The Response 2006: From sales leaders: 5.4 on a 10-point scale (where 1 is poor and 10 is most definitely). Ouch!

The Response 2010 and 2013: 6.5 out of 10 and 6.3 out of 10, respectively. About 50% of respondents replied with 6 out of 10 or lower.

The Question: "Sales leaders and sales managers are held accountable for the coaching, development and performance improvement of their staff."

The Response: Using our 8 out of 10 standard, 50% are held accountable, while 50% are not.

STRENGTHS

- Sales leaders are committed to helping their teams to hit plan.

- New sales team members are given time and encouragement for a few months.
- When sales managers are not rushed they are very consultative in coaching.

OPPORTUNITY

- Very good intentions to make time for coaching. With too much to do, it becomes the D priority ("Do it if I can").
- Rush to solve sales team issues which leads to us solving their problems.

DEFINITION

- Coaching is about questioning and listening a lot more than sharing your knowledge, ideas and suggestions.

FUSION LEARNING POINT OF VIEW

- Sales leader's job is *not* to create sales; it's to create salespeople. Coaching skills are critical to success.

GOAL

- **Measure talk time in coaching sessions — should be ⅔ salesperson, ⅓ manager.**
- **Measure frequency of coachee finding solution vs. manager — they should determine their own action plan 75% of the time.**

Are you catching fish for your salespeople or teaching them to fish?

PERSONAL EXPERIENCE – "DO YOU HAVE A MINUTE?"

Giving advice is easy, coaching is tough. My first workshop with managers was in 1992 and the skills taught then are similar to the skills taught today. In the classroom I can demonstrate great coaching with no trouble. But in the office, e-mails are stacking up, my calendar is back to back, my to-do list is long and I hear the knock, knock on my door. "Do you have a minute"?

What is my reaction, "Sure, come on in." What am I thinking? This is not going to be a minute; I have so much to do; hope this is a simple one; and quick. Let's get through this! STOP! This is a coaching moment and I need to be careful not to solve their problem, unless they are not capable of solving it on their own.

Solve it this time and they will be back, again and again. Why wouldn't they. Tough issue, go see the boss, they always know what to do. If you *solve*, you train them to come to you with issues. If you *coach* and allow them to solve for themselves, they will learn that it is not necessary to go to the boss for help with problems. When they do come, you will know it is a tough one that they really do need help with.

Coaching Skills

I have some great news! You have the skills that you require to be a world-class coach! You need to learn nothing new to be fantastic. Well, that's not quite true. You need to learn how to adjust how you use the skills that you already have to be even more successful than you are currently. As we all know, sometimes un-learning can be more difficult than learning.

Here are the five skills we've all learned to use when coaching (see Figure 2).

Figure 2: **Coaching Skills**

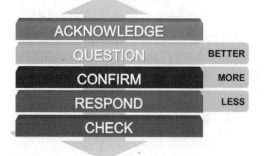

© 2014 Fusion Learning Inc.

1. **Acknowledge:** The use of verbals (i.e., Yes, Hmmm, Ah-ha, etc.) and non-verbals (body language like nodding our heads and making eye contact) *Acknowledges* to the salesperson that we are genuinely listening to them and we are interested in what they are saying.

2. **Question:** *Questions* help us gather information about the salesperson, their situation and their challenges. Ask them about their perspective. A good phrase to use is, "Tell me more about that."

3. **Confirm:** We use *Confirm* to help us make the progress of our discussion very explicit. In communication, messages can get lost. *Confirm* allows us to

ensure that we have correctly heard the salesperson, and that we have not missed any information they have given us. One way to *Confirm* is to paraphrase what we have heard. It is also our opportunity to create value by interpreting, integrating or summarizing information.

4. **Respond:** When we have engaged the salesperson and built trust, we earn the right to *Respond*. In *Respond*, we start to share our knowledge and our experience to assist the salesperson in solving their problem. We must be careful to not be too pushy. We want to add value with relevant advice.

   If through Questioning and Confirming they have solved their own issue, we may not need *Respond* or *Respond* might be more in the form of encouragement, as in, "Sounds like you have a good plan for this issue. I trust you to do a great job implementing it."

5. **Check:** The *Check* step in our skills helps to ensure the salesperson is comfortable with the conversation and allows us to pause from coaching. Often, we look for an emotional response from the salesperson by asking something like, "How are you feeling about our discussion?"

These are the definitions of the skills. You can see that you already have these. It is not the skill that is new — it is how to recognize your current behavior so you can determine the changes needed for you to improve as a coach. The good news? Small changes will lead to big results!

The Missing Skill?

One skill that may seem to be missing is *Listening*. Listening is really an outcome of *Acknowledge* and *Confirm*. As we acknowledge the salesperson through verbals and non-verbals, they "feel" that we are listening. When we say "feel," it is more of a "gut" feeling — they are not positive, but their instincts tell them we are listening. When we *Confirm* what we have heard, we move them from a "gut" feeling to being sure we are definitely listening. Help your salesperson "feel" you are listening through the *Acknowledge* skill but, most importantly, *prove* you are listening to them with the *Confirm* skill.

Let's talk about how most of us use these skills on a day-to-day basis.

Coaching Strengths

When we coach sales leaders, we often see that they are strong at the *Acknowledge* and *Respond* skills. They acknowledge that they are interested in what their salespeople are saying and they respond by sharing their knowledge and experience.

Acknowledge

Since childhood, we have been taught and we have built *Acknowledge* skills into our conversations. We can even use them when, in fact, our mind may be drifting. We may be thinking ahead, about our next comment or question or we may even be thinking about something unrelated to the discussion. Be careful during coaching with salespeople to use the *Acknowledge* skill genuinely; use it to show you are listening. This is a strong skill; use it to keep the salesperson engaged and providing you with information.

Respond

When we *Respond*, we get to tell the salesperson about our experience, how we would handle the problem and we get to show the extent of our expertise. We cannot help but be enthusiastic. This is our "comfort zone." We have lots of knowledge and when given this opportunity we will have lots to say, with lots of energy and lots of depth to share. This knowledge is great and salespeople love to see it, however, be careful. We need quality in our *Respond*, not quantity. We need to engage the salesperson in this discussion, not suddenly become the "expert" delivering our "expertise."

This great strength to *Respond* can become a great weakness if we rush to the step. We tend to hurry to the step if we have not asked enough *Questions* and when we fail to *Confirm*. If you are struggling with *Questions*, resist the temptation to *Respond* and, instead, *Confirm*. Most likely the salesperson will give additional information after you *Confirm* and this will help avoid moving to *Respond* too early. In summary, use the *Respond* skill wisely, in small quantities and after you have learned about the salesperson's situation, challenges and how they might propose to solve it.

If *Acknowledge* and *Respond* are typically strengths in the coaching skills of most sales managers, *Confirm* provides the best opportunity to improve our coaching, develop our salespeople and create a great sales culture.

Coaching Opportunity: Confirm

One key area to improve our coaching skills is our use of the *Confirm* skill.

Our natural tendency is to not *Confirm*. Some reasons for this are noted below.

- The salesperson already gave us the information, why repeat it?
- We will seem like a parrot repeating information and may upset the salesperson.
- We feel we've got it so we have no need to verify knowledge we have.
- We fear that we did not fully understand and if we *Confirm*, we will do so poorly.
- We are excited once we hear a salesperson's problem and if we *Confirm* it will slow us down.
- No time!

When we *Confirm*, one of four things will happen.

1. Salesperson agrees to the summary and feels good about being heard.
2. Salesperson will acknowledge our summary as correct but will additionally provide *New* and *Valuable* information (our summary triggered them to think of more information we need to know).
3. The salesperson clarifies a portion of the information in our summary.
4. Our summary is poor and the salesperson tends to shut down.

The first happens infrequently. When the salesperson accepts our summary, we can either move to *Respond* or we can *Question* more.

The second response, more information from the salesperson, happens frequently — and what a great outcome! We get new and valuable information, some we may never have received through questioning.

The third response happens often and will naturally lead to either more *Questions* or allow us to *Confirm* again, with the changes suggested by the salesperson.

Hopefully, the fourth never happens to us. We can help to avoid it by taking notes and by staying present when the salesperson is talking (i.e., not thinking too far ahead). The saying that most helps me to understand how to be ready to confirm is: "Hearing is involuntary. Listening is voluntary." Here is a mantra that I use to help me be a strong listener:

I must turn on the listening switch by being clear that I will need to confirm what I am hearing — I will pay attention and will take notes so I am well prepared to confirm.

The *Confirm* skill becomes one of our best ways to ask *Questions*. We summarize and it leads the salesperson to provide information. Remember, *Confirm* is not natural; in fact, it is natural to not use this skill. Push yourself hard to *Confirm* — you will benefit with new and valuable information from the person you are coaching.

For 20 years I have worked with leaders on how to most effectively use these five skills. To this day, I can still improve my use of the five skills. I am not a golfer but an analogy helps. These skills are like grip, stance and swing in golf. The very best golfers in the world, from Arnold to Jack to Tiger have great golf grip, stance and swing *and* they never perfect them. Coaching skills can never be perfect and we must strive to constantly improve.

Having an understanding of the five coaching skills, recognizing which skills are strengths and which are opportunities, and knowing that you will be continually working to improve them is good. Creating a great sales culture means having a plan of attack.

The Formula

So, let's revisit our goal — Question Better, Confirm More, and Respond Less. If you want to be a much better coach those six words are the formula.

Question Better

You are great at questioning; I know that is your perception. Most people by age 20 have been taught how to question so frequently that they can't fathom it not being a strength. Agreed! We are all good at it, but are we great? The best questioners in the world are reporters and talk show hosts. Who would dispute that Oprah and Dr. Phil are incredible at posing questions? Are you that good?

In coaching, remember the three questions that you want answered before you *respond:*

1. What do I need to know from the salesperson about this situation?

2. What has your coachee tried to solve this situation already?

3. What other solutions do they feel might be attempted that they have not tried yet?

Too often we rush to get some of the answer to the first question and then we lob a response that we hope will get them on their way. Often it does not because they have already tried that idea. We need to question better.

Everyone learns close-ended questions and open-ended questions. What we are not taught is the difference between "just okay" open questions and "great" open questions. Great open-ended questions we call Thoughtful Questions. A "just okay" open-ended question will get the coachee talking and sharing all kinds of information. We need this to get the facts. A Thoughtful Question will force them to think (Engage the Brain) or to share feelings (Engage the Heart). Let's see a few examples of Thoughtful Questions that could be used in a coaching conversation.

ENGAGE THE BRAIN

1. Compare this month and last month. What led to your greater success?
2. Analyze your recent sales success. What are the three key factors that led to it?
3. Define a great sales week with specific activity metrics.
4. Evaluate your current sales pipeline and steps you need to take to improve.
5. Map out your next 60 days, including a few key milestones.
6. If you were in my seat, what coaching would you give to you?
7. Outline a strategy and timeline to respond to the Request For Proposal that will be highly effective.
8. Substantiate why your bonus should be higher.

9. Consider the time when you were happiest in this role. What made you feel that way?
10. Describe the times in selling when you have the most energy and the times when you have the least energy.
11. Express a frustration you have that is impacting your sales productivity.
12. Give details of the steps you are taking to be more empathetic to your support team.
13. Measure your emotional reactions at work when you are happy and when you are stressed. What are the key differences?
14. Share how you feel on a great sales day and how you feel on a really tough sales day. (Follow-up question: What steps do we take to get more great ones?)

These are powerful questions. We must be careful when we use them that we have earned the right to ask them. They are also very situational and need to be developed for each coaching situation.

Looking at the list of 14 questions above, in your coaching today how many Thoughtful Questions did you ask? Questioning Better is not about more questions; it is about less questions that unearth more and better information. If you want to improve your questioning, start to build a repertoire of Thoughtful Questions. Create ones that work for you. Create ones you are comfortable with. Keep your list close when coaching so that you replace some close-ended and some open-ended questions with thoughtful ones.

When you ask Thoughtful Questions you will often get one of the following two responses:

1. "That is a great question." (Or a slightly different version might be "No one has ever asked me that before.")

2. "I am not quite sure what you are asking. Can you repeat the question?"

In both situations, the wheels are turning as they try to formulate a response. Be patient. It is a tough question and they need time to create their answer. Do not ruin a great question by interrupting their thought process. In the case of comment number two, you will need to repeat the question, but be careful, don't change it. Repeat the exact same question but say it a bit more slowly or a bit louder just to change it up.

THOUGHTFUL QUESTION HELPS COACH AND COACHEE

I once managed a sales leader who I found tough to engage in feedback. It often started well but it would turn confrontational, which would then require extra coaching time to try to unwind the tension. It was frustrating for me and for him.

In getting ready for a One-on-One, I prepared a Thoughtful Question to start our meeting, "Rate your ability to take feedback and explain."

He immediately responded, "Poor. And I have always been poor at taking feedback." He gave me a number of facts that really helped me to understand his point of view, including some very important details from his past. This led to a great discussion about how we could work together to make feedback work for him and dramatically improve my ability to coach him.

Confirm More

Let's replay the definition. "We use *Confirm* to help us make the progress of our discussion very explicit. In communication, messages can get lost. *Confirm* allows us to ensure that we have correctly heard the salesperson, and that we have not missed any information they have given us. One way to *Confirm* is to paraphrase what we have heard. It is also our opportunity to create value by interpreting, integrating or summarizing information."

Confirm is not repeating, it is summarizing *and* adding value. Help the salesperson to be really clear about the conversation you are having.

Let's review an example.

Sales Manager: Tell me about your pipeline.

Salesperson: I am really excited about the Real Estate Board (REB) deal. We have potential for multiple units there and my relationship with Graham is excellent. The study is completed and it is clear there is work that they are doing on the press that should be done on a copier.

Sales Manager: Great, REB is exciting. Tell me about what else is on your pipeline.

Salesperson: Well, I have been spending a lot of time on REB. ... I do have the deal at RR Financial (RRF) for two units that is supposed to go to the controller for approval and I've started the study at the Wales Federation Longshoreman (WFL) on that older piece of equipment to see if it is time to upgrade.

Sales Manager: In terms of timing, let's look at these three deals. Give me a time frame for closing on each.

Salesperson: Well, REB has a complicated structure for approval and they are still upset with us for the work our electronic division did a few years back so it is at least 90 days. RRF should be next month and WFL is just starting so it's hard to tell.

Sales Manager: Put that summary of your deals into a description of your pipeline.

Salesperson: I have three excellent deals that are capable of giving me a year that will be way over my plan.

Sales Manager: Okay, I like the optimism. Give me a more conservative view.

Salesperson: I have three large deals that are taking a lot of my time and if they do not come through, I could be in trouble.

Sales Manager: So we have two summaries — one paints a picture of an awesome year and one says we have a lot of eggs in a few baskets. Would you agree?

Salesperson: Yes, I must say I feel nervous when I think about how my year is going.

Sales Manager: So, what do you need to do right now to help with your nervousness?

Salesperson: I have large deals; I need some small, quick wins.

Sales Manager: How do you find those?

Salesperson: I think I need to do a thorough review of all my existing equipment in the field and see what is ready or close to ready for upgrade.

Sales Manager: Great, when will you do that?

Salesperson: I can come in this weekend and do the analysis so I am ready to visit potential upgrades next week.

Sales Manager: I like the plan. What can I do to help?

Salesperson: Check with me on Monday and review the potential opportunities I have identified.

Sales Manager: Will do.

What can we learn from this dialogue?

1. The salesperson solved his own issue (thin pipeline).

2. The sales manager had very good *confirm* ("So we have two summaries — one paints a picture of an awesome year and one says we have a lot of eggs in a few baskets. Would you agree?") that led to the salesperson to admit he was nervous, which led him to come up with a good action plan.

3. The sales manager did not take on work. She coached and encouraged, rather than solved or took on tasks.

4. A clear action plan with a check-in next week was developed.

5. Interaction created energy in the salesperson as opposed to increasing nervousness.

Respond Less

In our workshops we work really hard and practice a lot with participants on *Question* and *Confirm*. Invariably the same question pops up. "So, you are saying we should not use the *Respond* skill?" I love this question because it says they are buying in to making some changes. After surveying the group for thoughts, I always share my point of view.

"*Respond* is great. Just keep two rules in mind: quality not quantity and make a conscious choice to use it versus unconsciously going there because you are not sure where to go."

As a sales manager you have a lot of the answers. You were promoted or hired because of your expertise and skill. You always have two options when your team needs help: immediately share or see if they can create their own solution. If you choose immediately share, the possible sequence is this:

- Salesperson has issue.
- Salesperson asks manager what they should do.
- Manager provides solution.
- Salesperson implements.

That is one scenario, although it occurs very infrequently because most often the salesperson has already tried that solution. So, if you immediately share, the more typical sequence is:

- Salesperson has issue.
- Salesperson asks manager what they should do.
- Manager provides solution.
- Salesperson details how they already tried that, but it didn't work, etc.
- Manager (slightly embarrassed) asks one or two questions and tries to quickly redeem with idea #2.
- Salesperson details how they already tried that too, and it didn't work either, etc.
- This process can repeat several times and the salesperson will probably agree to a manager's idea that they

may have already tried as they do not want to embarrass them.

This sequence is also very time consuming with poor outcomes. It is not efficient or effective.
Seeing if they can create their own solution can be both efficient and effective:

1. Salesperson has issue.

2. Salesperson asks manager what they should do.

3. Manager ensures they understand the issue fully (tell me about it, what else should I know, what have you not told me that I need to know).

4. Manager summarizes issue and gets confirmation from salesperson that they have properly articulated.

5. Manager asks, "What have you tried so far to solve this problem?" (This essential question will help you to avoid giving them an idea they have already attempted.)

6. Manager asks, "What else might you try?" (Let's see if they can solve the situation — you will need to push them a bit as they came to you because they feel they have tried everything.)

7. If the salesperson comes up with a new idea, help them to articulate the plan, see how you can help and give them encouragement to go try.

8. If the salesperson cannot come up with an idea, now you know that they really need your help, you know what they have tried and can *Respond* with quality, not quantity.

The first two examples above are "solving" and the last is "coaching." What have you demonstrated today?

We are all programmed to solve issues. When presented with a problem, we immediately think, "What would I do to fix it." In our sales management role if we "fix," we are directing, not coaching, and we will be very busy. What's in it for me if I coach a team that will solve its own issues and only come to me when they are really stuck? And allowing salespeople to solve their own issues will lead to greater engagement. Great coaching Engages me!

Sales managers possess the five coaching skills — Acknowledge, Question, Confirm, Respond, and Check. To build a great sales culture, they need to lead their team to find the answers themselves; sales managers need to adjust how they use the five coaching skills by applying a plan, a set of goals to question better, confirm more, and respond less. Just as coaching requires both the sales manager and the salesperson to participate, feedback is most effective when it is collaborative.

Effective Feedback Is Not a Sandwich or a Seagull

THE RESEARCH

The Question: "Do sales managers have a model they use to provide feedback to their people?"

The Response: 56% said yes and 44% said no. Amazing, almost half of sales managers, do not have a model for providing feedback. This was an "aha" moment for us. People are giving feedback without a clearly defined way to do it.

The Question: We asked about frequency of feedback.

The Response 2006: 3% of leaders were providing regularly; 70% were providing feedback constantly or frequently

The Response 2010: 17% regularly — feedback frequency is accelerating; 80% were providing feedback constantly or frequently.

STRENGTHS

- Sales managers recognize that their teams need feedback to improve and be successful.
- Feedback is given on customer calls/meetings, proposals and time/territory management.

- Feedback is often a one-way conversation delivered from sales manager to salesperson. We know this from the exercise we conduct early in our sales management training sessions.

DEFINITION

The two-way Effective Feedback conversation has four easy-to-follow steps.

1. Ask the performer what they did well.
2. You add what you feel they did well.
3. Ask the performer what they will do differently next time.
4. You add what you would suggest they do differently next time.

FUSION LEARNING POINT OF VIEW

- Feedback must be a two-way conversation with self-discovery by the coachee being the first and most critical step.
- Sandwich feedback is a poor model. We must break the habit of using it.
- Seagull feedback is worse — fly by, poop and fly on. Never provide seagull feedback.

GOAL

Team members are so well versed in feedback, they can actually provide themselves with clear, actionable, realistic and balanced feedback on a daily basis.

Sandwiches are not good; Seagulls are forbidden!

PERSONAL EXPERIENCE — CONSTANT FEEDBACK WINS!

Fusion Learning grew 20% in 2012, 20% in 2011, 45% in 2010, 0% in 2009, 40% in 2008, and 45% in 2007. Our average annual growth rate is 28% and one of the most significant factors is feedback. When we hire new team members (all members, not just sales) we provide them with a two-page summary of what it will be like to work at Fusion Learning (affectionately known internally as "The good, the bad and the ugly"). Here is what we say about feedback:

> Growth and development is key in our industry, not only for clients, but for employees as well — you will receive constant feedback here, some you will like and some that is harder to hear — either way there is an expectation that you take it and act on it.
>
> We will be open and candid with you. If you are performing well you will know it and if you are not performing well you will receive feedback and coaching.

My personal belief is that our success in growing has a lot to do with feedback being frequent and helpful for our team. Everyone on the team knows that feedback is a four-step process and they know they will need to perform some self-discovery before they are given feedback by others.

Effective Two-Way Feedback

If you constantly praise your team members without suggestions for improvements, you will have an extremely confident, unskilled team. If you constantly suggest how they can get better without celebrating their success, you will have a skilled team that is lacking confidence. Balance in feedback is critical — not necessarily 50/50.

The tough task is breaking the habit of presenting to them what they did well rather than asking. You have years and years of history "giving feedback." Most often when you've received feedback, it was given to you — you were not asked. This first question in two-way feedback is the key to breaking previous habits. If you tell them, it is one way, but if you ask them, it is now two way.

SENIOR EXEC LEARNS NEW TRICKS

Recently I was working with a sales leadership team at one of the world's premier financial service firms. We had a pair of leaders demonstrate a coaching conversation and then the coach, Marty, was about to select another member of the group to lead the feedback for him. As Marty surveyed the 18 people in the room his eyes met those of the most senior executive in the room and before even being asked, Tom said, "Sure, I am happy to provide feedback."

Tom was a very senior leader who had been on major financial publication lists of who's who in asset management. I saw that Tom had notes written on the page in front of him and he was ready to "give feedback." A flash of the sandwich passed before my eyes and before he started, I jumped to my laptop and pulled up the image of the four-step feedback model. Tom gave me the "you interrupted me" look but then allowed me to remind him of the four steps. A bit reluctantly he followed the model.

He did an excellent job providing valuable, effective feedback. I was about to continue and decided instead to raise the question. I turned to Tom and asked if he would mind me posing a few questions about what just happened. He agreed. I complimented Tom on having notes to use in providing feedback, apologized for interrupting him at the start of the feedback and asked him if I had not interrupted him what he would have done. Tom was honest. "I was about to deliver the feedback — what I saw Marty do well and what I saw that he needs to change."

"So," I asked, "I pressed you to use the four steps. Be honest, how was it?" There was a pregnant pause. Essentially he could say it was better or he could question the model and potentially hurt the credibility of the workshop.

He said, "It was better." (Very large internal sigh from me as I began to breathe again.)

"Okay, how?" He was engaged and part of the discussion; it was no longer me delivering my message. He actually had some of the same ideas I had so I did not need to tell him. He brought it up and I reinforced it. This was a very, very intelligent and thoughtful leader and he validated the process.

In our training sessions, after we see the first demonstration of feedback (as mentioned it is usually one way — the sandwich), we review the four-step model. It is straightforward and with only five minutes of discussion, everyone understands it. I can blacken the projector and ask the group to share the four steps — no issue, everyone remembers. Then we put the group into a coaching exercise.

They view a coaching session and then the observer "leads" feedback. Guess what happens? Some success and a lot of feedback that starts with, "Here is what I saw you do well." The sandwich is so natural, it just happens. I will watch the group, and when I see a coaching conversation finishing, I stand by. When I see step two is where they start, I will ask them to pause. They look at me like a deer in headlights.

"Why did you pause me?"

"What are you doing?"

"Giving feedback."

"Yes, and what is the first step in Effective Feedback?"

"Oh, the model. I should use it."

Effective two-way feedback is common sense. The four steps are not a scientific breakthrough, but they are not common practice. Making these common practice will engage your sales team — feedback makes me better and if I am constantly improving, I'm engaged!

So, what to do? In training sessions it takes two days to get sixteen people so that they are consistently following the four steps. They will have four to seven opportunities to practice. When they return six weeks later for a follow-up, close to half will have fallen back to the sandwich. My belief is that we must truly understand the WIIFM (what's in it for me) of using two-way feedback versus one way. You will have to work hard to make the change and you and your team will greatly benefit from the change.

What's In It For Me (WIIFM)

One method provides the information needed for someone to improve — we have viewed their demonstration of a skill and we are able to tell them what they have done well and what they can do differently to improve. Why is that not sufficient? We believe what we formulate, what we are told is interesting but "Not Invented Here" kicks in.

Two-way feedback allows the salesperson to give you their views. They are part of the diagnosis and, most importantly, they are part of the solution. What will you do differently in the future? If you allow them to celebrate their success and you reinforce and add to it, they will give you their honest opinion of what they need to do differently next time. And if they say it, the chance of them implementing the ideas dramatically increases.

WIIFM? The content of the commentary will be very similar in one-way and two-way feedback, but it is the chance of change occurring that is dramatically different. You can "tell" them all you want in one-way feedback (insert picture of me hitting my head against the wall) or you can engage them in two-way feedback that leads to changes being implemented.

Once you are convinced of WIIFM, it is all about training yourself to start with step one. Here are the tips I give in our training sessions:

- Share the model with your team, and ask them to hold you accountable to use it.

- Make a visual model (see Figure 3) and put it where you will see it when coaching.

- Try engaging in feedback twice in one day, once as one-way and once as two-way feedback. Observe the change that occurs. The proof will help you!

- Convince yourself that "giving" feedback does not work; feedback must be a dialogue to work.

On the surface the four-step model makes sense. Knowing the WIIFM benefits is compelling. Seeing the proof of the success in a great sales culture is everything. Let's look at the model in more depth — step by step.

The Model

A quick recap of the steps before we tackle each individually (see Figure 3).

Figure 3: **Effective Feedback**

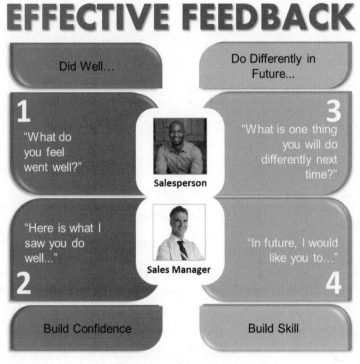

© 2014 Fusion Learning Inc.

1. Ask what they did well.
2. Add what you feel they did well.
3. Ask what they will do differently the next time.
4. Add what you would suggest they do differently next time.

Steps one and two build confidence. We need confident team members. Steps three and four build skill. All four steps create a confident, skilled and *engaged* sales team.

Step One: *"What do you feel you did well?"*

I ask the question and he starts to share. My mind drifts to, "What will I say he did well ..." Boom! I'm not listening to him. He might actually describe something he feels he did well but that I believe is something he needs to improve and I may miss it because I'm one step ahead.

When you ask the question, still your mind and engage them in discussion with:

- Why was that a strength?
- Give me an example.
- How did the customer react at that point?
- How else can you use this strength in other customer meetings?
- What might have happened if you had not done this?

Discuss their perceived strengths so that you are both clear that they are strengths and they are clear on how they will continue to use them in the future.

You can then ask them for a second strength and repeat or you can move to step two.

Caution: Many people will give you a laundry list when you ask for strengths. They are usually team members who struggle with self-diagnosis. They will recap the entire call instead of being specific about a strength. Slow them down and focus them with a more Thoughtful Question.

- Please pick the one strength demonstrated in that meeting of which you are most proud.
- What was your most brilliant moment in that meeting?
- If we asked the customer what sales skill they most admire in you, based on that meeting, what would they say?

Help them to narrow their focus to the one or two things they did best. They did lots of things well, what did they do *best*?

Step Two: *"Here is what I saw you do well."*

Your comments must be focused, specific, helpful and genuine. It is all right to agree with some of what they have said, but be original. What did you see that they have not mentioned? Engage them in the dialogue. "I liked when you challenged the customer by asking who they would show your proposal to. It opened them up and you were able to better understand the decision-making process for this important assignment. What was the customer's reaction when you asked that?" My feedback is delivered and now I have the chance to engage them and have them share in the celebration of this strength.

This step is very familiar to us as it is clearly part of the sandwich and we have had lots of practice. Be sure you still spend time on this step, even when you ask them. The most common issue I see with the four steps is that we have asked them in step one and we start to get lazy on step two. They need your view in addition to theirs; it will help them build confidence.

Let's look at an example of the first two steps.

Sales Manager: Thank you for allowing me to attend the client meeting with you. We need to discuss your action plan as a result of the meeting, but, before we do, I would like to have a feedback discussion with you. Is that okay with you?

Salesperson: Sure, always interested in improving.

Sales Manager: What do you feel you did well in that meeting?

Salesperson: Well, I was well prepared, I asked them a lot of questions, I was able to handle some concerns and we have clear next steps.

Sales Manager: That's great. I think I heard four or five things there. What would you say is the one thing you did the best?

Salesperson: I asked some great questions.

Sales Manager: I agree. What were some that stood out to you as most effective?

Salesperson: When I asked, "What do you predict will be the toughest parts to implementation?" And when I asked, "Describe how this project fits into your strategy for the next 3 years?"

Sales Manager: Both excellent questions — they really forced the client to engage and to think.

Salesperson: Thanks.

Sales Manager: You told me about those questions in preparation and it was great to see you fit them into the meeting. I am going to draw back to another comment you made about handling their concerns as the strength that I saw you demonstrate. (Transition from step one to step two.)

Salesperson: Sure.

Sales Manager: They expressed in their words and in their energy a concern about our ability to meet their aggressive timeline and I really liked that you did not jump to respond, but asked more questions. Do you recall when that happened?

Salesperson: I think we were talking about implementation and they seemed to question the size of our team.

Sales Manager: Exactly. I often see salespeople immediately say, "Don't worry we will be sure to have staff for your project." That can often lead them to worry. You turned it around and asked them if they had any concerns about our ability to deliver on time. They opened up to you and that then allowed you to allay their concern.

Salesperson: It did seem to go well. We built trust with them.

Sales Manager: Yes, you did. Let's move to look at a few things we could do differently in the future. (To be continued.)

Steps one and two build the confidence of our team members. Pause at the end of them and be sure they (and you) have celebrated their success. You will earn the right to go to steps three and four.

Step Three: "What will you do differently next time?"

A small question that opens up Pandora's Box. "I don't know and you are about to tell me so why should I share with my manager what I need to improve." This is a tough question for people. They are told to be strong and not to admit weakness.

Be patient and allow them to think. If they try to pass, ask the question in a different way.

- What would the customer suggest you do differently?
- What would you have done to get better or deeper information in the meeting?
- Take your time and replay a moment where you could have slightly adjusted what you did. What was that moment and what would the adjustment be?
- What was a moment in the meeting when you were uncomfortable and what caused that feeling?
- What questions did you not ask that would have been helpful?

Once they share, investigate their suggestion.

- Why do differently?
- What might have happened?
- How might the customer have reacted?

- How can you make sure you make the change?
- Tell me more about why you chose this change?

When you and they have investigated one change, you can ask for another and repeat or you can move to step four.

Step Four: "In the future, I would suggest ..."

As in step two, your comments must be focused, specific, helpful and genuine. It is fine to agree with some of what they have said, but be original. What did you observe that they have not mentioned? Engage them in the dialogue. Let's continue the feedback conversation from earlier.

Sales Manager: What do you feel you could do differently in the future?

Salesperson: Hmmm, I'm not sure.

Sales Manager: Think about one moment in the meeting that you wish you could have a do-over.

Salesperson: Oh, yeah, when they asked about the cost involved and I commented that we were a premium provider and we would definitely be more than the firm they previously used.

Sales Manager: All right, how would you handle it differently another time?

Salesperson: Well, what I meant to do was to ask them more than tell them. I have seen you in the past ask if they are looking for a premium solution or a regular solution.

Sales Manager: Yes, I think that could have worked well. What was the client's reaction to your comment?

Salesperson: It was okay. They are aware that we are a higher end solution so they were not shocked, but I wish I had used a question instead of a strong statement.

Sales Manager: No worries. Next time you will catch yourself and use the question.

Salesperson: Right.

Sales Manager: The one suggestion I have for you is I would like to see you driving the direction of the conversation. The customer sometimes does not know what they do not know and if you focus on what they want to talk about you may miss differentiating yourself from the competition. Where might you have directed the conversation?

Salesperson: We had prepared in advance to talk about getting buy-in across their leadership team and it was not raised in the meeting.

Sales Manager: Okay, was there somewhere you could have raised it?

Salesperson: Ah, maybe when we talked about their worry over our ability to deliver on time. It could have been a nice place to talk about their team.

Sales Manager: Yes, I like that and how would it have helped us?

Salesperson: We would get to hear more about who is on side and who may not vote in favor of our proposal.

Sales Manager: Exactly. And we would have been able to help them strategize for those who may not be bought-in.

Salesperson: Thanks, that is helpful.

Sales Manager: Thanks again for including me. It was a pleasure to see you in action.

Steps three and four build the skill of your team members. Pause at the end of them and be sure they (and you) are committed to the changes you have discussed in these steps. Because the salesperson spent the time and energy to come up with their own insight and "aha moments," they are far more likely to become more skilled — starting now.

Common Issues with the Four Steps

Amazing what we can learn about people's ability to understand themselves. Using this model for many years, it is clear to me that many people have excellent self-perception and diagnosis capability. And many do not!

Let's look at some common issues and solutions with the four-step process.

They Share a Strength You View as an Opportunity to Improve

One of two things could be true here. It is a strength and they are correct or it is not and you will need to raise it when you get to step four. We need to determine which it is. Your coaching skills are critical here. They raise it as a strength and you want to say, "Oh no, I see that as an opportunity." Don't go there! That would be you responding and jumping to step four.

Instead, ask a question. "Tell me more about how you see that as a strength?" or "Please give me an example of how you demonstrated …?" Discuss the "potential" strength to determine if it is or if it is not. If they cannot explain or back-up the strength, you need to stay in step one rather than move into step three or four to outline what they felt was a strength is an opportunity. Say, "We will discuss this later. Let's go back to something else you feel was a strength."

Let's review an example. The scene is a feedback discussion after you attended a customer meeting with one of your sales team members.

> **Manager**: Thank you for letting me attend your meeting today. Let's spend 5 minutes on feedback for you. Sound good?
>
> **Salesperson**: Sure.
>
> **Manager**: Tell me one thing you feel you did well in that meeting?
>
> **Salesperson**: Well, I asked great questions, I was well prepared, the client got very engaged and they have asked me to prepare a proposal for them.
>
> **Manager**: Great. I heard four things there. What is the one thing you did best?
>
> **Salesperson**: I asked great questions.
>
> **Manager**: What were some examples of great questions?
>
> **Salesperson**: Hmm … I asked, "When will you implement this change?" and they gave me some great details. And I asked, "Will you be the person who signs the contract?" and they said they would after reviewing with senior management. I also asked them if they were happy with our work on the last project and they gave us some positive feedback.

Manager: Okay, you gave three examples of your "great" questions — when will you implement, will you sign the contract and were you happy with our work. What type of questions are these?

Salesperson: They worked well. I guess they are close-ended questions. I know we have talked about them before.

Manager: Let's leave questioning for a minute. What is a behavior you had in the meeting that you are really proud of?

I chose this example as salespeople often cite questioning skills as a strength. They interpret getting some good information from the client as proof that they asked great questions and that is not always the case. As managers, we often agree that they had great questions when it is not true. Not only are we giving weak feedback but we are encouraging them to continue with poor questioning. A strength can be "I got great information from the client" (not being said is "despite asking poor questions").

You Ask What They Did Well; They Say Nothing

This response usually occurs after a poor meeting/demonstration of skills or with rookies. They are deflated; you probably had to help. They struggled. Step one is critical at this time. They need a boost of confidence. You can jump in and move to step two but it will be hard for them to hear as they are discouraged and thinking of all the things they could change. Stay in step one and allow them time to think about the things that did go well, not all the things that did not.

Ask them again, "Take your time and think through the meeting. Share with me one thing that worked well." Pause, allow silence, allow them time and they will share a strength. Take time to explore it to make sure they really believe it was a strength. "What worked well with that?" Or "How did the customer react when you did that?" Or "What information/emotion did that generate for you?"

You will know you have been successful when their body language moves from disappointment to open. They are not jumping for joy but they are acknowledging that some things did go well. You will also have to help with your "did wells" in step two. They need to be real and genuine and they need to help with confidence building.

You Ask What They Did Well; They Move to What They Could Do Differently

Salespeople who are highly critical of themselves and those who lack confidence are quick to jump to what they could do differently. They are wired to look for change not to celebrate success. You need to stop them in their tracks. Interrupt them and remind them we are celebrating success and we will have an opportunity to discuss changes in a few minutes.

Let's review an example. Again, the scene is a feedback discussion after you attended a client meeting with one of your sales team members.

> **Manager**: Thank you for letting me attend your meeting today. Let's spend 5 minutes on feedback for you. Sound good?
>
> **Salesperson**: Sure.

Manager: Tell me one thing you feel you did well in that meeting?

Salesperson: Nothing. I just ...

Manager: (interrupts) Hold on, we are going to look at strengths first and you did have a number of strengths in the meeting. What is one thing that went well?

Salesperson: I am not feeling great about it.

Manager: I understand that this was not your greatest meeting but let's first focus on the things that did go well. Think about a time in the meeting when the client was engaged. What did you do to lead to that?

Salesperson: Hmm ... I asked, "What will make this new process difficult to implement?" and they gave me some great details.

Manager: I agree, I really like that question. What led you to ask it?

Salesperson: In my preparation for the meeting I talked with someone I know who works there and they gave me some good background. It led me to believe that this will be a tough change for the organization.

Manager: Nice — a second strength was your preparation for the meeting. What else did you do to prepare?

Salesperson: I spent time on their website, Googled for recent information and I prepared some questions, including the implementation question.

Manager: Nice work on preparation and with the implementation question. Let me add two things that I saw you do well.

The feedback conversation starts with a dark cloud and we help to clear it out. The salesperson is feeling bad and, if we immediately go to the negative, they will end up feeling worse. We have had a good discussion on strengths and they are seeing that despite it being a poor meeting there were some strengths. Of course, it is critical to then discuss the changes needed — it was a poor meeting and we need to help them make changes to avoid difficult meetings in the future.

They Suggest a Change You Feel Is a Strength

Similar to when they list a strength that you feel is an opportunity, they might be right and they might have the wrong perception. Be careful not to jump in with your view (that would be using *Respond*), and instead ask them why they feel this is an opportunity.

They might be able to show you, in which case it belongs in step three or they might struggle to support why it is an opportunity. Help them to see that it is a strength and that they should continue to do it in the future. If they cannot back it up, it is acceptable for you to share that you see it as a strength. Once you determine it is a strength, be careful to ask again for one thing they would like to improve. It is important that we fill box three so that we build skill in addition to confidence.

Timing and Balance in Feedback

We have four steps in Effective Feedback. Do we spend 25% of the time in each? No. Definitely not!

Different people have different capacities for feedback and different abilities to assimilate information. Those lacking confidence need more in steps one and two. Those who are very confident but lack skill need more time in steps three and four, but be careful that it comes after reinforcing confidence in steps one and two.

Although we have taken a full chapter on this critical topic, do not feel that the four steps of Effective Feedback need take long. I can watch a coach for 15 minutes and then have an excellent four-step feedback conversation with clear action steps in less than 3 minutes. Yes, at first, it may take you a bit longer but once you are used to the model and your team members know they must participate, 3 minutes can work very well. That is not to say you should only spend 3 minutes — often it needs to be a 10-minute conversation.

Coaching skills and Effective Feedback are essential abilities for a sales manager. You must be constantly working to develop and improve your techniques and practices to create a great sales culture. Skills without disciplines will only go so far. Clear and well developed systems will bring coaching and feedback skills to the fore that will feed into a robust attitude for an *engaged* sales team and a winning sales culture!

PART III

SALES MANAGEMENT DISCIPLINES

Structure sets you free! This section of the book will seek to ensure you have a very formalized structure for each sales management discipline. It sets you free because, if you have a process, the discipline is in consistently exercising it. In the absence of structure, each time you go to coach or manage you will spend time thinking about the "how" and the "what." With structure the "how" is set and ready for you to insert the "what."

We will suggest the use of some forms in managing your salespeople. Let's be clear, the notion of forms is not one we all get excited about. When we first developed our process for One-on-Ones, I steadfastly resisted the use of a form. That was too structured. I laid out my page the same every time and my notes were in the exact same places but to me it was still free form. Luckily, one of our clients at the time was also a personal friend. We worked with his sales force over a 3-year period to improve productivity. He kept asking that we create a One-on-One form rather than only teaching the process. I refused. He created it himself. I saw them put it into action and I was converted. Forms work.

Sales management disciplines are about quality and quantity. By quality we mean they add value to your salespeople and they create productivity in your organization. When we are first hired in client organizations we sit in on sales meetings and One-on-Ones. We often see the sales manager putting a "tick in the box." Quantity is there, value is not. The goal must be that we "check the box." The team or the individual being coached is much better off from the time spent with them. They will adapt some of their behaviors and their results will improve. Engage your team with excellent sales management disciplines.

You are doing good things in managing already. Please look for the tips in this section that will help you go from good to great. Remember, progress, not perfection.

CHAPTER 4

Good Versus
Great People

THE RESEARCH

The Question: "Our organization does an effective job of recruiting and retaining high-quality sales professionals."

The Response 2010: 6.6 out of 10

The Response 2013: 6 out of 10. Only 28% responded with $^8/_{10}$ or higher with 40% answering $^6/_{10}$ or less.

The Question: "Each member of the sales force is highly effective in the communication skills needed to secure sales and build strong client relationships."

The Response 2010 and 2013: $^{6.5}/_{10}$. Only one in four respondents felt their salespeople rated $^8/_{10}$ or better in selling.

STRENGTHS

- Every sales organization has great salespeople — those who end up delivering beyond our expectations.

- How do we consistently create an organization that has high performers and where high performance is the norm, not the exception?

DEFINITION

ROOMr: Having great people has three critical components that lead to one outcome.

- **R:** **Recruiting** — strive for only great; be patient to wait for that person
- **O:** **Onboarding** — the time needed to become proficient in role
- **OM:** **Ongoing Management** — do not assume high performance; everyone needs to be managed on a consistent basis.
- **r:** **Retention** — we use a small "r" as this is the outcome

FUSION LEARNING POINT OF VIEW

- "If you want a good company, hire good people. If you want a great company, hire great people." — *Robin Sharma*

GOAL

ROOMr that works so well that you have 0% unforced turnover.

Don't expect retention, create it!

PERSONAL EXPERIENCE —
UNFORCED TURNOVER

At Fusion Learning, we have had an incredible ability to limit unforced turnover. Before I give details, I need to admit that we have experienced turnover that is much too high. Let me explain.

We are a small organization. We started in 2000 and in our first 10 years, we had one person who we would classify as "unforced turcnover." I personally managed him and I was completely shocked when he resigned. I consider this one of my top failures as a manager.

During that 10 years we had a lot of turnover. There was some form of mutual agreement or we felt it was not working and we helped the team member to move on. As I say, the only thing worse than a poor hire is hanging on to that person hoping they will make it. How have we been so successful? This chapter will share some of what has worked for us (as do all the chapters in the book).

Let's discuss great versus good. Great is constantly improving; good is happy to stay constant. Great is a team player; good is an individual contributor. Great embraces feedback even when it is tough to hear; good hears feedback and forgets it. Great is humble; good has a strong ego that can get in the way. Great is intense and focused while still being able to laugh; good lacks intensity. Great brings smiles to their managers' face; good can cause management frustration. It is important to note that salespeople don't arrive at sales organizations as great — they arrive with the *potential* to be great. They must work hard and the manager must help to bring them to great.

I was having dinner with my good friend Robin Sharma and we were discussing our two companies. I was expressing to Robin how tough it was to hire and how we made hiring mistakes too often. That is when Robin shared the quote from above. "If you want a good company, hire good people. If you want a great company, hire great people." From that day forward, Fusion Learning would hold all potential hires to the standard of "we need to believe they will be great." At a recent team gathering celebrating a 10-year anniversary at Fusion Learning, Tim Magwood, founder of Fusion Learning, looked at the assembled group and said, "There is not a good person here ... you are all great!" The team was very happy he finished the sentence!

ROOMr

A short story on how we came up with ROOMr. We were having our quarterly Advisory Board Meeting and we were studying the high turnover I mentioned earlier. Why did our hires often end up as turnover because the potential great person turned out to be average? We listed every hire in the previous few years and started to study their evolution.

What steps did we take to hire them? How were they brought into the organization? How long until they were successful? If unsuccessful, how long until we or they made a decision that Fusion Learning was not the right place for them? What happened between hire and success or departure? The major aha moment from the exercise was the length of time that passed from the moment of hiring to success in a role. It was often a long period from hire to recognizing that they would not be successful. We realized that onboarding was the Achilles' heel for us.

We determined that onboarding was too casual and too short. In order to have a great hire we would need excellent recruiting, strong and lengthy onboarding and disciplined ongoing management from day one. If we got these three right, we would get retention. Since creating the acronym, many of our clients have also admitted that onboarding is the part of ROOMr that most troubles their sales team.

We ended up with three steps that led to our ultimate outcome — retention (see Figure 4.1). Here is the acronym in action — ROOMr:

1. **Recruiting** — strive for great only and be patient to wait for that person.

2. **Onboarding** — ensure vigorous support to help new team members learn their jobs.

3. **Ongoing Management** — once onboarded, do not assume high performance, and once high performing, do not assume it will always continue. Everyone needs to be managed on a consistent basis.

... ultimate outcome ...

retention — too often we demand retention instead of creating it.

Recruiting

Recruiting is one of the toughest tasks as manager and it is very stressful. We need to fill the position and we are scared to make a mistake. We try to mitigate risk by engaging others, using tests and checking references ... and we still have hiring errors.

ROOMr

Recruiting + Onboarding + Ongoing Management = retention

RECRUITING	Strive for only great and you must be patient to wait for that person before hiring.
ONBOARDING	Determine the time needed to become proficient in role and ensure vigorous support to help new team members learn their job.
ONGOING **M**ANAGEMENT	Do not assume high performance, and once high performing, do not assume it will always continue – everyone needs to be managed on a consistent basis.
rETENTION	We use a small 'r' as this is the outcome. Too often we demand retention versus creating it.

© 2014 Fusion Learning Inc.

We have found that there are three phases in the recruiting process.

1. Hiring Criteria

2. Sourcing

3. The Interview — affectionately referred to as *The Gauntlet*

Hiring Criteria

Often we begin recruiting when we are not clear what we are looking for. If you are going to spend time to recruit, let's be sure the specifications are clear. What are the job responsibilities? What behavioral characteristics are you looking for? Are you looking for an experienced hire or are you willing to train?

Sourcing

This step has gotten easier with the Internet. Access to candidates is easier than it has ever been. That can be a double-edged sword as it can be hard to find the diamond in the rough. At Fusion Learning we use search agencies. They use the Internet to source and the fees we pay are high but they save us a ton of work when they are managed properly.

My rule is "three strikes and you are out." Recruiters can send me candidates on a contingency search (we only pay if they are successful) but if they send me one who is not properly qualified and not at least a "good" candidate, it's strike one. We will discuss the candidate and how they should not have made it past the screening process. We repeat if it happens a second time. Third time and they are off the search. I will not see candidates from them for that role. To be clear, a good candidate who we like but not enough to hire does not count as a strike. Essentially, there are "greats" who we hire (or make our best attempt), "goods" who will go through some steps of our interview gauntlet and "okays" who will not go beyond a first interview.

Interview Gauntlet

This step, in our opinion, is where most organizations go wrong. The process is too emotional and too simple. We look for who we like and who we feel would fit. We trust a few people to interview and momentum can often take the day — the first interviewer really likes them, tells this to the second interviewer who uses this bias to see what they like and our rose-colored glasses are clouding the interviews. Recruiting takes time and when we are on candidate number six or eight or ten, our frustration can lead to only seeing the good. Interviews must be about removing all bias and determining ability to be great in the role.

Fusion Learning's process has three key components.

1. **Interviews:** All candidates from administrators to executives will meet and be interviewed by at least eight members of our team. We do solo interviews, pair interviews and meal interviews. We have junior team members interview senior candidates and vice versa. Interviewers have pre-assigned behaviors they will investigate and critical job accountabilities that they will probe for examples. Every opinion counts. After the interview, the hiring manager will receive a list of Green Flags (things they like about the candidate), Red Flags (cautions and concerns), a score out of 10 (1 = Poor, 10 = Strong) and a Yes or No for the question, "Would you Hire?" At the first interview, the candidate will be interviewed by two or three team members. The second interview has five or six members asking questions. When a third interview is required, it is a second chance for the hiring manager and key executives to have a final look.

2. **Behavioral Test:** We like an objective third-party test. We use Caliper (www.calipercorp.com), which has a very thorough online test, followed by a phone consultation with one of their assessment consultants to discuss the candidate. The consultant knows us so they are looking at the behavioral assessment and fit with Fusion Learning's Values/Culture. The test doesn't determine hiring; it is one tool we use in making a decision. There are many tests available. Find one that works for your organization and use it consistently. Our research shows 60% of sales organizations have a behavior test in place.

3. **Job Simulation:** Interviews are used at every organization. Assessments are used at many. Simulations are a hidden gem in the hiring process. Only 26% of sales organizations in our survey currently use this technique. For every position you hire, a job simulation can be created.

    Simulations allow you to see how the candidate will perform in the job. It is all fine to talk about how the interviewee would approach the job, how he or she has tackled tasks in the past, and what his or her strengths and weaknesses might be. Seeing them actually handle a situation is most telling.

    Here are some examples we have used.

    • Desktop Publisher — We have two parts to our test. First a typing test. This provides data on speed and quality/attention to detail. Second is a Microsoft Office test to show skill in Word and PowerPoint. This demonstrates capability with the software, attention to detail and speed (we have a time limit and give more work than can be accomplished so we see how far they get).

- Accounting Clerk — The candidate inserts American Express statements into an Excel worksheet. One month is presented as an example and the second month is to be prepared.

- Salesperson — This is a prospecting simulation. The candidate is assigned a prospect profile, time to prepare and then they place the prospecting call to the hiring manager who is in another office. At least two members from our sales team listen to the call and prepare feedback. The candidate is given feedback and then asked to incorporate it into a second attempt. This simulation tests prospecting skills as well as the ability to take feedback. If we do not see incorporation of ideas from the feedback in the second call, it is very unlikely we will hire that person. Being open to learning is a critical behavioral competency we hire on.

- VP, Finance — We take financial statements and allow the candidate 15 minutes to study. We ask them to prepare questions and insights. You know the key items that stand out, see if they pick them out. A strong candidate should provide some insight that is helpful.

- Client Solutions Consultants — The candidate is given information about a program that needs designing. That candidate is asked to create a design flow, agenda and pre-work. Key in this simulation is the discussion following the task where the candidate has the opportunity to explain his/her approach to design and the choices that were made. We also use the pre-work note to test writing abilities, a key job accountability.

Each of these simulations has been used at Fusion Learning. They are an essential tool in hiring. If they can't wow you in simulation, how will they wow you on the job?

When a candidate has passed the interview gauntlet it is time to hire. We have one last step at Fusion Learning — "the good, the bad and the ugly." A simple two-page note that we use to make sure the candidate is ready for what will come. It has not led to anyone refusing the job, but it has helped once they are onboard and going through the early stages of learning their new role.

SO, YOU'RE THINKING OF JOINING THE FUSION LEARNING SALES TEAM? A COUPLE THINGS YOU SHOULD KNOW ...

It is a great place to work, with lots of wonderful people and awesome development opportunities! It is a fast-paced, highly engaging, collaborative environment where you are supported and challenged and success is celebrated. The client list is fabulous, with opportunities in a number of different industries ... all of this you likely know from your online research and conversations that you've had with our team so far.

Some things you should know about what we expect.

- We have values that are very important to us and guide our actions in how we work together and with clients. We recognize our team members regularly on how they demonstrate these values and expect these to be guiding principles for our entire team.

- Extremely fast-paced — think of a "fast-paced" work environment you've experienced and multiply it. We move fast around here and you must be ready to keep up!

- Extremely high expectations when building your book of business — you are expected to meet and exceed your key monthly metrics. This includes number of calls made, first meetings and subsequent meetings booked and held, number of proposals sent and deals closed (although we know it takes some time to build your book of business — you will be expected to be driving a lot of activity).

- We prospect, collaborate and share successes as a team. We also go on joint calls/meetings together. In short you will be supported to succeed by your fellow sales team members.

- Attention to detail is key to us — you are expected to go above and beyond to ensure that all client proposals and presentations are well thought out and accurate. If they are not they will be handed back for you to correct.

- Growth and development is key in our industry, not only for clients, for employees as well. You will receive constant feedback here, some you will like and some that is harder to hear, but either way there is an expectation that you take it and act on it.

- We "walk the talk" — we "live and breathe" our sales models and are known as being the best consultative sales people in the industry. Our expectation is that you will contribute to our great sales culture by completely embracing the Fusion Learning way. There is lots of structure in our sales environment and this is not for everyone.

- Unlike many other sales environments, the expectation is that you are in the office from 8-5 every day, unless you are going out to meetings.

- Work/Life balance can be a challenge in this environment — nobody "watches the clock" around here. The expectation is that you are responsive and deliver high quality to each of your clients, which can sometimes mean early mornings and/or late evenings (especially during RFP season).

- Please know that we are a performance-based culture. You must perform to succeed — and you will be well rewarded for it!

- We are measured and coached based on monthly metrics. Your monthly performance bonus/commission will be based on your achievement of these goals.

What you can expect to receive.

- We will be open and candid with you. If you are performing well you will know it and if you are not performing well you will receive feedback and coaching. Should your performance continue to suffer, we will work with you on a performance plan.

- Our goal is that your pay is in the top remuneration in the training industry. There is no ceiling on pay. Be prepared for onboarding that takes about 15 months and higher productivity to take 18 to 24 months.

- We care about you. We will equip you to succeed.
- We work hard and play hard. We like to have fun. We have a great office. We often eat lunch together. We celebrate our success often. We have taken our team and spouses to Cancun, Jamaica and New York City. We once flew our team by float plane to an island in Georgian Bay for a planning retreat and celebration. Our annual holiday party is not to be missed!

Fusion Learning is an amazing place to work ... for the right person! The expectations are high, as are the rewards. Please consider all of this carefully before making your decision to join our team.

Onboarding

In the ROOMr equation, onboarding is the toughest. How do we get a new person up to speed so they are producing and successful? Large organizations that can hire a "class" can create a shared group experience but even then success is far from guaranteed. We struggled with onboarding at Fusion Learning and believe it has been a reason for high turnover in the past. Our Fusion Learning Sales Culture Survey also indicates others are struggling with the question. "We are effective at onboarding new members of our team" scores 6.2 out of 10 on our surveys and 51% of sales organizations give themselves a 6 out of 10 or less.

One year ago we decided to break the back of this issue. We, like many organizations, were viewing onboarding as the first 3 months of employment — did they arrive, get settled, make some friends and does it "feel" like they will be successful. Wrong definition!

Onboarding is the time period from hire until they are fully competent in their job. For more junior positions this is a shorter time frame, while for senior positions this can be a year or more.

Once our definition changed, we determined time to success. We created 3-6-9-12-15 months as time frames for our key positions. Three months for desktop publishers, 6 months for Fusion Learning facilitators, 9 months for project managers, 12 months for consultants and 15 months for salespeople. Just recognizing the time frame helped us to get clear and to set clear expectations.

With the timeline clear, we created onboarding plans. Each onboarding plan is a written document and each employee receives the appropriate plan upon accepting the position. The plan outlines what the new hire is expected to be able to demonstrate by a particular month in their position. These are progressive plans that articulate the minimum standard you must achieve to progress and be successful. Some get ahead of the schedule, some take longer but it is a clear measure of success. Managers are available to coach but the heart of our onboarding plan is they are owned by the new team member — you are accountable for your own success — we are here to support.

Here is the onboarding plan (see Figure 4.2) for salespeople joining Fusion Learning (with plans for other positions within Fusion Learning in the background).

The plan has five categories.

1. Attitude and Strategy
2. Skills
3. Knowledge
4. Healthy Funnel
5. Activities and Results

Figure 4.2: **Onboarding Plan**

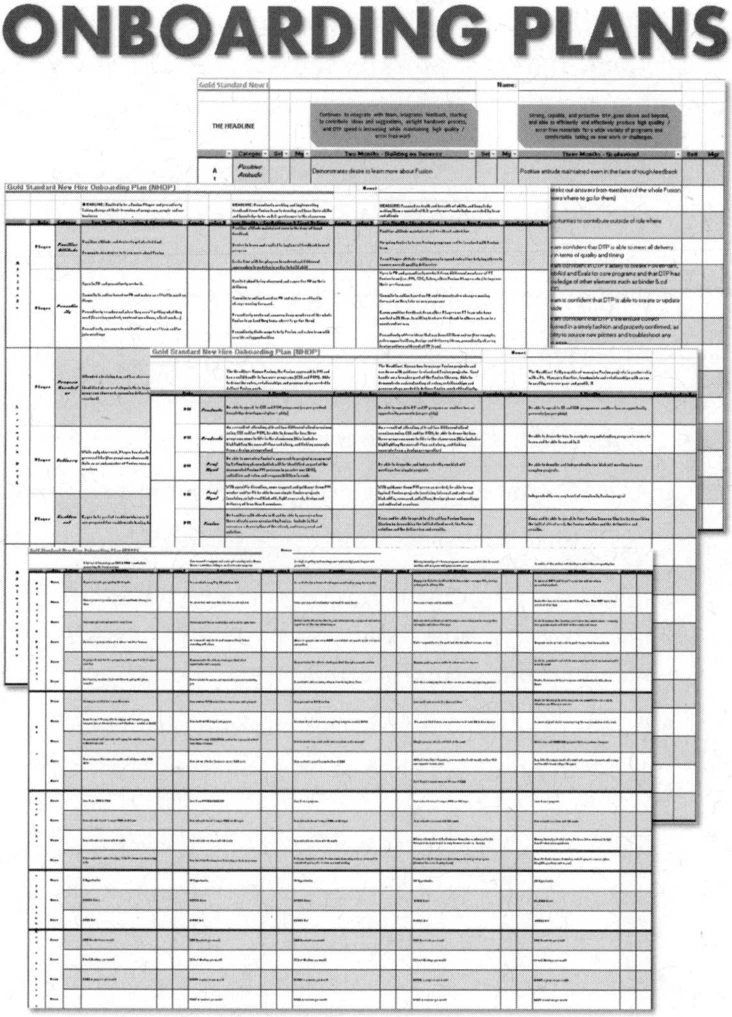

ONBOARDING PLANS

© 2014 Fusion Learning Inc.

Each of the categories has three to six descriptors of what the team member must be able to demonstrate to show proficiency at the 3-, 6-, 9-, 12- and 15-month marks. Graduation occurs when they are largely able to demonstrate proficiency across the onboarding plan (progress, not perfection). The descriptors for the five time categories are as outlined.

- At 3 Months: A high level of knowledege on consultative selling skills and practical sales management (two Fusion Learning solutions); comfortable prospecting the Fusion Learning message.

- At 6 Months: Able to research a company and quickly get a meeting with a senior buyer; comfortable talking to most of Fusion Learning's solutions.

- At 9 Months: Adept at getting first meetings and conducts high quality dialogues with prospects.

- At 12 Months: Strong knowledge of all Fusion Learning solutions and demonstrated ability to convert meetings into proposals and proposals into closes.

- At 15 Months: Achieves activity and results metrics and is strategic in where they spend time.

So here is the interesting data from our research. Of sales organizations in our Fusion Learning Sales Culture Survey, 78% have onboarding plans that are 6 months or less, with 41% being 3 months or less. Only 4% have an onboarding plan of greater than 12 months. Selling sales training is definitely a tough sales job but is it that much harder than most? Are we crazy to have a period this long for onboarding or are other organizations underestimating the time required. We are only 1 year into our journey on onboarding so I pose more questions on this topic than provide answers. *Engage*

Me II will need to expand on this topic (can't blame a sales guy for planting the seed).

We also celebrate graduation. It is hard work to complete an onboarding plan and when you do we want you to know you have achieved an important milestone. We have had two graduation parties in the last year and all graduates have received a graduation gift.

FOUR OUT OF FIVE AIN'T BAD

Here is one story from our onboarding work in the last year. We created the five plans and then we compared our current employees against the plans. We realized that on four of the five plans that our current team would have some work to do to graduate. We had to create some lunch and learns to help the team. The key topic area was product knowledge. People did not know our programs nearly as well as was needed from both our sales team and our consulting team. For the fifth plan, we realized most would easily graduate; we had made the plan too simple so we had to revise it to include more stretch targets.

Ongoing Management

This book is all about ongoing management. Every member of your team needs coaching, management and recognition. Low performers need it, okay performers need it and high performers need it too. The goal of ongoing management is participation rate.

*Participation Rate is the percentage of your sales
team members who are at or above plan.*

For a sales team, participation rate is easy to calculate. If you have ten people and four are above their sales plan on a YTD basis, you have 40% participation. My experience is that this statistic is often not studied. Why? Sales managers are measured for making their quota. If I have to deliver $100 million, my job is to get my ten salespeople to deliver on average $10 million each. Some will give me $15 million and some will give me $5 million, I just need it to add up to $100 million by the end of our fiscal period. This system actually incents me to keep average performers. You may only deliver 50% of your quota but that is better than 0% if I manage you out.

When we first began discussing participation rate, we assumed most sales leaders could hit 100% of their revenue plan with a participation rate of about 65%. We recently conducted a survey and were surprised at some of the results. Ninety-three companies shared their 2012 results on participation rate and how well they performed against their revenue plan. The surprise, one-third of companies had a participation rate above 70% yet only 60% of these actually made their revenue plan. Surprising and it would seem almost mathematically impossible. We reached out to some of these companies and uncovered the factors that could lead to the surprise.

- Open territories that did not have salespeople so these areas are not accounted for in the participation rate but do hurt revenue.
- Turnover that leads to experienced salesperson being replaced by junior salesperson — they achieve junior

goal but company needed senior sales production to hit plan.

- Plan involves some stretching that is not in the salesperson's targets.

- Major accounts/national accounts that have few salespeople and a big target can hurt overall revenue success but not impact participation rate as they are a small percentage of the sales force.

So, unfortunately we could not prove that a high (70%+) participation rate could guarantee above-plan performance. Yet, participation rate is key to above-plan performance. The survey did provide some insights, just in an unexpected way. Sixty-three of the companies had participation rates of 60% or less. Of those 63 compannies, 6 made their revenue plan (less than 10%). The conclusion?

A participation rate of 60% or less will give you a 10% chance of making your revenue plan. You must aim for a high (70%+) participation rate to have a good chance of making your revenue plan, although it is not guaranteed.

So, why do we tolerate poor performance? What stops us from having tough conversations? We are nice! We do not want to rock the boat. Hope is our strategy. They will improve soon. I don't want to get a bad reputation. The list of excuses is long and the amount of denial (not the river in Egypt) is high.

Four Performer Categories

Performance can be evaluated on two criteria — behavior and results. Assessing whether they are or could be delivering results is fairly straightforward — it's a math problem. Behavior is the one component that many sales managers overlook, but it will tell you if the person is following the set processes and in line with the company values.

At Fusion Learning we assess both criteria and we look at performers in four categories.

1. **High Performers:** Deliver above what is expected on a consistent basis. They also follow process and exhibit the correct values. (Deliver results and behave correctly.)

2. **Coachable Performers:** Behave in a way that is consistent with values and processes and we are confident they will get results with continued coaching — but results are not yet where they need to be. (Behave correctly but results not at 100% yet.)

3. **Tough Performers:** Deliver results but tough to manage. They cut corners, they leave a trail of destruction or some variation on that theme. We hang on because we "can't afford to lose them." Or can we? What collateral damage is being caused? What are they saying to others about accepted standards of behavior. We tend to say one more chance. They need to fall in line or we will find a way to do without them. (Deliver results and behave poorly.)

4. **Poor Performers:** Team members who are not meeting expectations and are not really following behaviors that we know will lead to success. Colleagues or customers may like them but they are not focused on being successful. They are "filling" the role. (Poor results and poor behaviors.)

The OM (Ongoing Management) of Performers

We all have stories of Tough Performers. The story goes something like this.

They deliver and are really great but I get frustrated at times as they don't follow accepted norms or guidelines. I talk to them and they promise to change, and they do for short times but typically slip back quickly. I allow it as I don't want to rock the boat and I can't afford to lose them. Of course it gets worse so then I do have to intervene and at some point my frustration or that of other team members hits a peak and we decide to part ways. They scream on the way out, "You'll regret this!" And as they say it, I am really worried that I will.

The happy ending — we do get by without them. Not only that, we find some of the hidden issues that they had managed to bury or the work that they were not doing that they should have. People who we thought would support them say, "That was the right decision." And for them — they move on to something new and in a lot of cases are better off for it. Let's look at my examples — like you I have a lot of these.

TOUGH PERFORMER STORY: A WIN-WIN SOLUTION

Early on at Fusion Learning we had three contract facilitators who we used to deliver our training programs. We relied on them to bring our learning alive in the classroom. One of the three, and arguably our best facilitator, was a Tough Performer — awesome in the class, but very tough to manage. He complained about what he was paid, wanted extras, towed his line more than the company line and saw those that he trained as his customers and us as a necessary evil in the middle (despite us finding the business, signing the contract, managing the relationship and designing the learning, etc.). We delivered tough feedback to him and he would improve in a minor way for a short period. Then it hit!

We found out he intended to do work with one of our clients directly, despite that being against our contract. We discussed and his view was, "You can't do anything to stop me." Legally we could but who wants to go there. The business partners met and it was clear — time to make the tough decision. Losing one of three facilitators and your most experienced was a very scary proposition, but it was the right thing to do. We parted ways, with him delivering the "you'll regret this" speech. Guess what? Best decision ever.

We never looked back. Never missed them. It pushed us to find other facilitators and pushed us to have more bench strength in the future so we would never be in the same position. We also jumped on issues with contractors sooner, enforced procedure when they tried to avoid it and we were not afraid to make tough decisions early. We learned and we improved.

And for the contractor, he did more of his own business and did not work as a sub-contractor. Good outcome for them and good outcome for us.

When we make a hire we are excited. We have searched and after some tough going we find our person. They come on board and we see roses; they are new and they are shining. Then the honeymoon ends. Things are not perfect, they are not learning as fast as we had hoped. We coach, we mentor, we encourage and we provide balanced feedback. That is how it all went when we hired an administrator a few years back. Great hopes but they struggled.

COACHABLE PERFORMER STORY: THE SEVEN PAGES

Three months in and I was really liking her as a person, but her work was not meeting standards. Balls were hitting the floor versus staying in the air. Coaching had been provided but we were small and we needed people to learn on the job. So, time for what later became known as "the Kevin talk." That is the polite version.

The net of the tough conversation (to be discussed later in this chapter) was we like you, we see potential, but you need to immediately make changes, get organized and deliver against the potential you have ... or (else) this may not be the place for you. To her credit, she took the conversation to heart and returned the next day with seven pages of notes on her reflection of the first three months, the conversation from the day before and, most importantly, the action plan they proposed to be successful.

Reaction to a tough conversation is the number one indicator of the future and seeing that document showed me that she intended to fight to stay. The outcome — seven years later she is a critical member of our team, she has been promoted twice and her income has tripled. We held our first annual shareholders awards last year — nominations were from peers — and she was nominated by over 20% of her colleagues, easily being the first ever recipient of the Shareholders Award. Coachable Performers are great to have and, with the right support (and maybe a Kevin conversation), they will blossom to high performance.

The OM for Managers

How does your team stack up and how does that relate to your stress and workload as a manager? In an ideal world, you would have 100% High Performers. Neat concept, most likely not going to happen. We can get close but circumstances and life will come along. What is the next best thing? One hundred percent High Performers and Coachable Performers. You have those who are performing and those who are doing the right things and with some coaching they will deliver results. This is attainable, although from my experience, not the norm. Managers who have close to 100% in these two categories will have a manageable workload. They will feel in control and will see results from their efforts at ongoing management.

Now let's move closer to reality. Most leaders will have some Tough Performers and some Poor Performers. Let's say you have ten direct reports and two in these groups. Not bad, manageable. Say it is four of ten — life is tougher and you have tough moments on a daily basis. Six out of ten and it is probably tough to get out of bed in the morning. This ratio is very important. In essence, it is the "how tough is my job as a manager" ratio.

The table would play out like this.

- 20% Tough and Poor Performers = Life is Good
- 35% Tough and Poor Performers = Stressed and a bit stretched
- 50% Tough and Poor Performers = Firefighter

- 65% Tough and Poor Performers = Dismantle the team (HELP!)

THE SEVEN PAGES — REVISITED

A few years back I had a manager on my team who had three direct reports. She had 100% Tough and Poor Performers. When we labeled the team it was "part time, inexperienced, wanting to be elsewhere."

She was a good manager, so you might ask how her team got there. I would say time and circumstance led to the team. We were using contracts since we were growing fast and wanted to be careful of how many full-time staff we added. We decided that the team needed to change. The goal: full time, dedicated and excited. The timeline (admin positions) was 4 months.

She made it. The team was completely changed. We moved from one full-time and two contract people to three full-time employees. One contractor did not apply; the manager helped him to see this was not part of his long-term vision. One contractor applied and was not successful. The one full-time person was managed out. Two of the three hires are still with us and have had numerous promotions. They became full time, they were dedicated and they continue to this day to be excited.

You can change your team, you can do it in a reasonable amount of time and it will make your life easier. Her stress went from high to low with the change in her team and the performance dramatically increased.

Part of the story just shared is the notion of "horses for courses." This has been one of my most important, and at times painful, lessons in growing our business. When we were a start-up we needed some generalists or Jacks/Jills-of-all-trades. We found a couple and they were terrific. As we grew, the list of tasks for one person started to narrow and we had to develop our generalists to be more specialists. In some cases we were successful and in some cases the generalist was best as a generalist and we were forced to part ways — horses for courses. Being a member of a fast growth, performance-based firm has also led to those who keep up and those who are great when hired but tire of the pace — horses for courses.

Let me be clear. The people I am describing have been a big part of our success and we are so fortunate to have encountered them and, at a certain point in their/our development, the perfect fit went away and a tough decision had to be made. A really, really tough decision. In my story of the manager of three, I remember that when the manager and the one full-time person who was managed out met, and the manager delivered the message, the employee said, "You look more upset than me. It's okay. We knew this was coming."

OM Before the Tough Conversation

Let's take one step back and talk about what happens before we get to the tough conversation — which is a lot! As detailed in this book there is plenty of coaching and feedback. There are monthly (minimum) One-on-Ones. There is observational coaching with feedback. There are sit downs to try to help. If these day-to-day routines are not working, we hit a point where a performance conversation is necessary.

Your direct reports have the right to understand if they are not meeting your expectations. A performance conversation has five key steps.

1. Set a clear standard and set milestones of performance for the direct report.

2. Inform the direct report where they are not meeting the standard and set milestones.

3. Give the direct report the opportunity to meet the standard and set milestones.

4. Offer assistance to meet the standard and set milestones.

5. Advise the direct report of the consequences of not meeting the standard and set milestones.

I am not going to go into great detail in this discussion. Our finding is that managers know how to do this — the issue is getting up the nerve. Hope springs eternal and I will avoid this talk at all costs. Why? I believe the pain of keeping them is less than the pain of the conversation and the pain of managing them out. This is an urban myth. Have the conversation as soon as needed. Those who want to be with you will step it up and improve (see the Seven Pages story earlier in this chapter). Those who are not capable/not interested will show very quickly (weeks not months) after the performance conversation.

So what happens when you have had the performance conversation and things do not improve? It is now time for the final warning. Please consult with your HR team to effectively handle the final warning and how to go your separate ways if that is required.

We have reviewed ongoing management, including the importance of participation rate and how to performance manage, let's look at retention.

retention

It was mentioned at the start of the chapter but let's refresh. Retention is a small "r" as it is an outcome not an activity. We all understand that engaged employees stay (are retained) and disengaged employees leave or, worse, they are internal terrorists.

We want retention so we measure engagement once per year. The results come out and we see our employees are not as engaged as we would like. Teams are formed and action plans created. Lots of excitement and energy with great intentions. Changes are made and we wait for next year's survey which comes out and we see a little improvement but not near what we hoped. We repeat the process. If this sounds familiar, it is because it is a cycle we see with our clients frequently.

Here is the new idea and the theme of this chapter.

Recruit with vigor and hire only "great" team members.

Onboard the "great" not until they are comfortable, but until they are competent in the role.

Ongoing Management starts on day one and must continue on a daily, weekly and monthly basis.

Your reward is built-in retention, rather than a holy grail you chase once per year after receiving survey results that are not where you want them to be. *Engagement* starts with strong recruiting, continues with excellent onboarding and must always have ongoing management.

In our three-step process that leads to an ultimate outcome, we see that each step has a process within it. By far, ongoing management is the most involved and time-consuming component, and you will see ghosts of this topic throughout the book. Whether it's coaching skills in Chapter Two, delivering Effective Feedback in Chapter Three or the high priority of One-on-Ones that we'll be discussing in the next chapter, making positive steps in this area will reflect winningly for your salespeople and you as sales manager. How can you have a great sales culture without great people and great managers? Make coaching, feedback, One-on-Ones part of your regular sales management discipline.

One-on-Ones
Are About People
(and Performance)

THE RESEARCH

- 97% of managers are holding One-on-Ones.
- 85% hold them monthly or more frequently and 27% hold them weekly.

The Question 2013: "How valuable are your One-on-One meetings?"

The Response: Sales leaders rated them 6.9 out of 10; 16% rated them as 10 out of 10; and 40% gave themselves a 6 out of 10 or lower.

STRENGTHS

- Managers are holding One-on-Ones.
- Attention to task and business results is front and center.
- Deal coaching will absolutely happen and assists the salesperson.

OPPORTUNITY

- One-on-Ones lack structure. They tend to have a laundry list or what is the hot issue/big deal focus.
- Salespeople come prepared with a "good story."
- Both manager and salesperson see them as a "necessary evil" versus business critical. Frequent rescheduling further demonstrates their lack of importance.

DEFINITION

- A scheduled, formal, private meeting between a sales manager and a salesperson held monthly at a minimum.
- Manager must prepare in advance (our system: 5-10 minutes) and the salesperson may also be asked to prepare (try to minimize their prep time).

FUSION LEARNING POINT OF VIEW

- One-on-One meetings between salespeople and their sales managers are a fundamental right of an employee and a fundamental need for success as a manager.

GOAL

One-on-Ones are so valuable that if a manager cancels or misses the meeting, the salesperson reschedules it.

As Woody Allen said, "Showing up is eighty percent of life."

PERSONAL EXPERIENCE —
NO CHAPTER AT CHAPTERS

When we set out to create learning on one-on-ones, I visited my local book store, Chapters. I thought I would see what the books on management had to say on the topic.

I went to the sales management section (about 50 books), which was beside the management section (about 300 books). I opened the books and looked for the chapter on one-on-ones. Guess what I found — none. Not a single book had a chapter devoted to what we think is a very important sales discipline. The best I could find was a few pages.

And the inspiration for this book was born, along with my dedication to creating a world-class system of one-on-ones.

I hold One-on-Ones with my six direct reports the first Friday of every month. My team has access to my calendar to schedule so in bold letters it is written: PEOPLE DAY — No client work/meetings. To me this is sacred time. I connect with my key leaders, celebrate the previous month and help set them up for success for the next month.

Are they nice, fluffy, soft conversations — far from it. Does my team love them and come in hollering "yippee" — absolutely not. Would they rather it be canceled — not a chance. Are they tough conversations — not always but frequently. Same story, different month — no way, because if it were we'd need to have a very different conversation (see Chapter Four: Good Versus Great People).

The business world is tough and people need to get out

of the trees and look at the forest periodically. For me, I want the One-on-One to be that time.

The Typical One-on-One System

As we saw in our opening, all managers are holding One-on-Ones. But as we also saw, they are regarded as a necessary evil — by both salespeople and sales managers alike. However, some sales managers recognize the value of these meetings and up the ante, as my second sales manager did.

THE SHELL GAME

One big issue with One-on-One's that especially happens when they are held too frequently (weekly) is the "same story, different week" syndrome.

I began my sales career at Xerox, which had excellent sales disciplines. We had a One-on-One for 30 minutes with our manager every Monday morning. My first sales manager was an excellent salesperson who, as frequently happens, was promoted to be an average, at best, sales manager. Our One-on-Ones were very friendly, we discussed accounts, I would get a few ideas, told him what he wanted to hear and then returned to what I was planning to do. Value add to me, to him and to the business was minimal.

In retrospect, we were playing the shell game. We would move the shells around looking for the pebble that was there, although in reality it was not. I came "ready to play" with my stories on accounts so when he lifted the shell, the pebble was there. It was predictable, fine and a necessary evil. Two years later, a new manager was assigned to our team. No worries, I was ready for the shell game, part two.

The first meeting was similar with one difference; he took notes and put them in a file folder with my name. The second week, the game started again, but when he inquired on an account (lifted the shell), I told a similar story to the previous week. He referenced his notes and I started to squirm a little. No worries, he said. "Let's discuss how you are going to move it forward this week." Silly me, I showed up for week three and tried a similar story. He was still nice about it, but I realized the game had changed and I needed to follow through on my commitments as they would be checked the next week.

No more same story, different week. I needed to move things forward and be accountable to the plans made or I would be exposed at my One-on-One. One-on-Ones became important to keep me accountable and to move the business forward. My manager was a great salesperson and a great manager who helped his team win business by staying focused and accountable.

A traditional One-on-One would meet the following criteria:

- business focused,
- past focused,
- tactical, and
- a single meeting.

At Fusion Learning, we pride ourselves in having a world-class One-on-One system. It is:

- business *and* person focused,
- *future* focused,

- strategic first *and* tactical second, and
- a *series* of connected meetings.

The system relies on three key components.

1. Standard Agenda.
2. Manager Preparation before meeting on a standard form (see Figure 5).
3. Manager File for Employee.

A High Priority Activity

As you review the system keep in mind that One-on-Ones need to be a high priority activity that adds value to you *and* to the employee. Our experience is that One-on-Ones are often just reviews of current activities/deals, which has led them to be considered a low priority activity.

The analogy I think about for One-on-Ones is the forest and the trees. The strategic part is the forest — how is the salesperson, how are they feeling, what is their overall performance, what are the main strengths and the main barriers getting in their way. I always want to start at this strategic level. Then we move to the trees, the tactical — key deals that need attention or planning, activity levels, prospecting activity, pipeline health, etc. This chapter will help establish a system for conducting world-class One-on-Ones. It will be your responsibility to integrate what you learn into your management style so that you are seen as conducting world-class One-on-Ones.

ONE-ON-ONE FORM

Salesperson: _____ Sales Manager: _____ Date: _____

Big Picture:

Opening Question: _____

①—②—③—④—⑤—⑥—⑦—⑧—⑨—⑩

[ ]   [ ]

1. Salesperson Green Flags:	**3. Salesperson Red Flags:**
a.	a.
b.	b.

2. Sales Manager Green Flags:	**4. Sales Manager Red Flags:**
a.	a.
b.	b.

Activities/Results:

Help Needed (Sales Manager):	**Salesperson Action Plan:**

© 2014 Fusion Learning Inc.

Standard Agenda and Form

The standard agenda ties into the first opportunity — lack of structure. Employing an outline for One-on-Ones will help you maintain focus, be consistent, and your team member will know what to expect. The standard agenda for a world-class One-on-One has six items.

1. Big Picture
2. Green Flags
3. Red Flags
4. Customers/Pipeline/Activities/Results
5. Help Needed
6. Action Plan

The agenda is suggested as a guideline to help you have a productive conversation. The form is engineered to help you structure the conversation, to prepare for the conversation and to make notes of the conversation. You will need to customize the agenda/flow to match your business and your style. We will discuss timing for each part of the agenda as we detail how to conduct it. The full agenda is covered during a productive One-on-One.

While there are three components to the system, the agenda is by far the most detailed piece for successful One-on-Ones. That doesn't mean the other components — manager preparation and manager file for employee — are not important, but they will flow from working through the stages of the agenda.

A caution: If you have not had many One-on-One meetings in the past, it will take some time to establish a routine with your sales team. They will only take these meetings as seriously as you demonstrate them to be. They will actually try to get out of the meetings until you can prove to them that they create value. If you are not creating value, stop, reassess and plan in advance how you will make the time you spend together very valuable for you and your salesperson.

1. Big Picture

The first topic of discussion is the salesperson. You want to avoid jumping into their most important meeting or a pressing matter. This meeting is your chance to connect with them strategically and tactically.

For the "Big Picture" question, we recommend using a 10-point scale, letting the salesperson know what constitutes a "1" and a "10." Then ask them to rate themselves. Utilizing this scale is an incredible tool to quantify what is often qualitative. One question by itself is good but what is very powerful is the ability you have to chart progress over time, to understand how good something is or how change is not happening.

BIG PICTURE SURPRISE!

I was coaching a sales leader on conducting world-class One-on-Ones and as we prepared for an important meeting with a member of his sales team, we determined the Big Picture question to be: rate your sales performance in the last quarter on a scale of 1 to 10, where 1 is poor and 10 is great. When I asked him what she would say, he remarked, "7 or 8." When I asked his ranking of her performance, he put her at a 5 out of 10.

We prepared for the meeting based on this perception. When we went into the One-on-One he asked the Big Picture question and waited for her response. She thought for what felt like 1 minute but was probably 10 seconds and responded. "I think I am a 3 or 4." WOW! Talk about the two of us looking like deer in the headlights. We were very prepared to help her see where she had an inflated perception of her performance and now we were caught dead in our tracks. So, what happened?

The manager spent the next 10 minutes helping her to see that she was not performing that poorly and to increase her confidence. What should have happened? Stick to the plan with Big Picture — accept her rating and ask her to give details.

Help her to create a realistic picture of what she is doing well (in this case a short list) and where she is missing on expectations (a long list). Whether she is a 3 or 4 or 5 is not relevant. Can she outline clearly her strengths and her opportunities? With a good list, we can help to set a good plan to improve. Use the Big Picture to quantify but then allow the performer to help back up the number.

The Process

Let's look closer at the process for Big Picture (the conversation should take 5-10 minutes) and then we will discuss some best practices.

For those performing at or above expectations you might want to learn how challenged, happy, successful or stressed they are using the 10-point scale. Why go here? This person is critical to your personal success, your team's success and your business's success. High performance does not guarantee job satisfaction or employee engagement. Trust me, I learned this the hard way.

ASK THE RIGHT BIG PICTURE QUESTIONS

In my first 10 years of leading Fusion Learning, I have only had one person resign. Please don't take this the wrong way — we have turnover, too much in fact, but all of it, except this one case, was mutual or "desirable." What happened?

I was doing my One-on-Ones and I was asking the Big Picture questions but not the right ones. I had asked this High Performer to rate how stressed he was and he said 9.5 on a 10-point scale (1 was not at all stressed and 10 was totally stressed). A few months later, he resigned. Hindsight asks, "Why did I not ask if he had considered looking for greener pastures which anyone with that level of stress must be considering?" Instead I tried to help to lower the stress.

My goal is to make sure this never happens again and Big Picture questions of High Performers can help me make sure they are not highly successful flight risks.

High performance does not mean perfection. Often we take the accomplishments of High Performers for granted. "Of course Samantha is happy; she was just selected as salesperson of the year for the second year in a row." Beware of assumptions and be diligent to hold One-on-Ones with all of your team, not just those who are struggling.

For those performing below expectations you will ask them to rate their performance on a scale from 1 to 10 where

1 is poor and 10 is outstanding (superior, superstar, top performer). Frequently those performing below expectations will rate their performance higher than it is. A salesperson whose performance you would rate at a 4 or 5 will probably rate themselves as a 7 or 8. A salesperson whose performance you would rate as a 6 will rate themselves an 8. The process to help better align the salesperson's "perception" with your view can be straightforward.

1. Share the performance scale with the salesperson and ask for their rating. Be patient and get a number from them (do not share your view, work from where they are). The performance question can be overall sales performance or it can be more specific like prospecting activity, client meeting activity, proposal quality, closing rate, etc.

2. Ask, "Why did you rate your performance this way?" Note all positive contributions in a column on the left and rate any areas they mention as below expectations or where they are not performing in a column on the right (you are creating a "balance sheet" of performance with assets on the left and liabilities on the right).

3. Ask questions that build the non-performance column on right. Ask questions that get them to share where they have not spent time and should have; targets that they are not paying attention to and are behind on; internal or client issues; actions agreed to but not followed though on, etc. They tend to leave this information out and they need questions from you to get them to voice where they have problems.

4. Summarize all aspects that they have mentioned as performing and all areas that you have elicited as non-performing. Then ask, "Does this summary of performance match the rating you gave?" Have them readjust the rating to be more reasonable. They do not have to match your rating. The goal of the discussion is to have them see they are performing below their perception.

5. Ask, "How do you feel about this performance?" Allow them time to respond even if it's a bit uncomfortable.

6. Ask, "What do you plan to do to change your performance?" Help them put together an action plan and write it into the "Action Plan" box of the One-on-One form.

7. Ask, "When we next meet, what will your rating of your performance be?" If they set the improvement goal too high, help them to adjust to a realistic goal and set them up for success in attaining this improvement target.

Best Practices

All notes from the Big Picture discussion go in the Big Picture box on the One-on-One form. What are some best practices for Big Picture?

- Vary the questions you use from meeting to meeting and tailor it to the individual.

- If time permits, you can use two Big Picture questions.

- It is not about the rating number; it is about the dialogue that results from the number.

- Their perception is reality. If their perception is off, you telling them will probably not change it. You need them to articulate the story behind it and, with your questions, help them to more properly share the full story that will then allow them to alter their perception.

- Be careful of asking "feeling" questions in the Big Picture. "How do I feel about my performance? I feel great as I am new and I really should not be expected to do much." If asked to rate my performance, I might not pull the rookie card!

2. Green Flags (Build Confidence)

The discussion of the Big Picture will give you insight into the salesperson — what they think about their performance, how that perception aligns with your rating, and how are non-performance items regarded. This will lead to items two and three on the agenda. The Green Flags section of the One-on-One is your chance to recognize strengths in the salesperson's performance.

The Process

This is the second part of a world-class One-on-One agenda and should take less than 5 minutes of conversation. You want to first ask them for their Green Flags and then you add the Green Flags you observed.

1. Ask the salesperson for one thing they are proud of since your last One-on-One. Allow time and make note of the Green Flag on the form. Ask them for a

second item they are proud of. Discuss their Green Flags, give praise and allow the salesperson to celebrate their success. Talk about these points and have them live in their success for a few moments (even if they are a Poor Performer). If they raise a Green Flag where you are not in agreement, ask them to give details and back up why they feel it is a success. If they can, it is. If not, say, "Let's table that idea (meaning we can discuss in Red Flags). Please give me a different thing you are proud of in the last week or month."

2. Shares two things you are proud of that the salesperson has accomplished since you last met. If your Green Flags (prepared before the meeting) are the same as the salesperson's, let them know that. Be sure to give specifics of the Green Flag and again allow the salesperson to feel proud. Do not rush this step. Be careful to make your feedback about thanks and celebration not connected to the Red Flags that will come next.

This discussion is important as it will build the *confidence* of the salesperson. You will recognize this step as similar to the "Did Wells" outlined in the Effective Feedback chapter (see Chapter Three). These are the first two steps of Effective Feedback with one difference — when giving Effective Feedback it relates to a specific performance event — in the One-on-One it relates to the last period of performance (i.e., the last week or last month since we had a One-on-One).

Best Practices

Comments are captured in the Green Flag section of the One-on-One form. Some best practices for Green Flags are outlined below.

- If the salesperson raises a Green Flag that you do not agree is a strength or success, inquire (use Acknowledge, Question, Confirm) to learn more. If they are able to substantiate, it is a Green Flag. If they are not able to prove it, ask them to leave it aside (we can talk about it in Red Flags) and to give a different Green Flag. Do not immediately go to the Red Flag section — we need to complete Green Flags before we go to Red Flags.

- Try to limit them to two Green Flags (maximum three) as we are not looking for the complete list of everything they did, but for the two things that they are most proud of.

- When surprised by a Green Flag, make sure you get to the reason they are proud. You did not see this as a proud moment for them so it is a great time to understand something about them that you did not previously recognize.

- Be careful of celebrating the same success on multiple occasions. Salespeople might tend to celebrate when they hear they will get the business (month one), when they sign the deal (month two) and when the revenue starts to deliver (month three and beyond). Look back at last month and comment, "I totally agree that is a big Green Flag and we had that last month. Let's talk about this month."

3. Red Flags (Build Skill)

While the Big Picture discussion will lead to both Green and Red Flags, be sure to take time to acknowledge and celebrate the Green Flags. Don't rush to get to the Red Flag section of the One-on-One where you will discuss areas needing improvement in the salesperson's performance.

The Process

This third part of a world-class One-on-One should take less than 5 minutes of the conversation. You want to first ask them for their Red Flags and then you add the Red Flags that you have.

1. Ask the salesperson for one thing they want to improve in the next few weeks. Allow time and make note of the Red Flag. Ask them for a second thing they want to improve. Discuss their Red Flag areas, and help them create an action plan for improvement. Be certain it is a realistic action plan and note the key elements in the salesperson's action plan section on the bottom right of the world-class One-on-One form.

2. Share two things you want the salesperson to improve in the next few weeks. If your Red Flags (prepared before the meeting) are the same as the salesperson's, let them know that. Be sure to give specifics of the Red Flags and help the salesperson create an action plan for improvement. Comments are captured in the Red Flags section of the One-on-One form.

This discussion is important as it will build the *skill* of the salesperson. You will recognize this step as similar to the

"Do Differently" outlined in the Effective Feedback chapter (see Chapter Three). These are the third and fourth steps of Effective Feedback with one difference — when giving Effective Feedback it corresponds to a specific performance event — in the One-on-One it corresponds to the last period of performance (i.e., the last week or last month since we had a One-on-One).

Best Practices

Comments are captured in the Red Flag section of the One-on-One form. Some best practices for Red Flags follow.

- If the salesperson raises a Red Flag that you feel might be a strength rather than an opportunity to improve, inquire (use Acknowledge, Question, Confirm) to learn more. If they are able to substantiate, it is a Red Flag. If they are not able to prove it, reinforce that it might be more of a Green Flag or at least not something that needs to be emphasized in what they need to do differently to be more successful. Ask them for a different Red Flag and be patient to wait for their answer.

- Try to limit them to two Red Flags as we are not looking for the complete list of everything they can do differently, but for the two things that they must focus on to create the largest gain in performance.

- When surprised by a Red Flag, make sure you get to the reason they want to focus on this item. You did not see this as an opportunity for them so it is a great time to understand something about them that you did not previously recognize.

The first three items on the agenda have dealt with focusing on the salesperson and their performance within the business and how those assessments relate to the future goals for the salesperson and the business. That was strategic. Now it's time to get tactical. This section of the One-on-One is much more familiar to you as it is probably the majority of what you currently do in your One-on-Ones.

4. Sales Activities/Results

The fourth agenda item of the One-on-One is where you get tactical. You've had the strategic discussion (Big Picture, Green Flags, Red Flags) and now you discuss ways to help them be successful in their territory, in their meetings and sales. This section will go into details and will consume about half of the time you spend in your One-on-One. Be careful to keep this as a discussion.

The Process

In our observation of sales leaders, this section is an area of strength. Managers are ready to roll up their sleeves and salespeople will come looking for help on their most pressing matter or the deal(s) that requires help. Be careful, when they are struggling; they are also looking to use this time to avoid the more strategic review of how they are not meeting expectations. Do not allow them to take you to this part of the conversation until you have held the strategic discussion (Big Picture, Green Flags, Red Flags). You also want to utilize your coaching skills and your success formula of Question Better, Confirm More and Respond Less as you conduct this and all parts of the One-on-One.

The trick in this section of the One-on-One is to be all-encompassing versus deal focused. The deal manager will spend all of this time (and potentially all of the One-on-One) on deals. Salespeople are happy to do this as then you are only talking about the future and their weaknesses are not being exposed.

ONE-ON-ONE MISDIAGNOSED

A sales leader that I managed asked me to help in coaching one of his team. "He is struggling setting up meetings and needs someone to listen in on his prospecting calls." No problem, happy to help.

As I sat down in his office, I immediately noticed that his desk was a mess. When we started to look at the Customer Relationship Management (CRM) database, I noticed his computer had lots of files and programs open. The first call he was about to make was to a small IT service company — not in our target market and not someone he should be calling. When he went to access the information on the potential client he pulled up an Excel file. My immediate question, "Why are you using Excel instead of the CRM?"

"Don't worry she is also in the CRM." Ouch, nothing like doing double entry. He then opened his CRM to show me she was there. Next, we discussed "A" accounts versus non-target accounts. He claimed to have called all his "A" accounts so he was now focusing on non-target. I asked to see his "A" accounts.

For the first one I picked he had done a nice job reaching a senior leader who had given him two people to contact and he had a meeting scheduled with one of them. When I checked to see if he had circled back to inform and thank the leader — No. The second "A" account we looked at (and a good account that he should be contacting), he had no contact names so had made no attempt to contact them (in his defence, they had only recently been added to his list). For the third account, there were lots of contacts, lots of reach-outs yet there were many contacts that he had not even attempted to call. My conclusion and my coaching to him was that he needed to get a much better system for prospecting and be focused on "A" accounts.

I tell this story as it illustrates what happens when you are a deal coach. You are not in touch with what your people are doing and it leads you to not understand why they are not being successful. The time to understand what is really happening is in your One-on-Ones. The manager who asked me to support his salesperson had no idea what the most pressing issue was. He was correct that the salesperson needed help on how to make calls, but before we fixed that issue, he needed help to call the right people.

Let's look at the many areas and ways to ensure we do a deep dive on what is happening with members of our sales team. The great news is that technology has dramatically enhanced our ability to understand at a glance what our sales team is up to. At Fusion Learning we utilize three critical systems so that even if I am out of the office for a month, I can log-on and see what has happened. First is salesfore.com. It shows activity, forecast and results. Second is Microsoft Outlook Calendar, which shows appointment activity in a chronological view. Third is our timesheet system which permits me to see how all time is spent both during the week — what is recorded on Outlook and what is individual activity.

Before we look at results, I always like to review activity. We must know what activities our salespeople are engaging in to be able to plan a tactical effort in our One-on-One. In sales there are really five critical tactical activities.

1. **Research on Prospects:** This can be industry research, company research or key contact research. (Special Note: LinkedIn has revolutionized how you research contacts and if your sales team is not using it, start now.)

2. **Prospecting:** Phone calls, leaving voice mails, sending e-mails or using social media to contact decision makers all count as prospecting.

3. **Meetings:** We measure two types of meetings — first meetings with a prospect and all subsequent meetings. Why? If you only measure meetings, the sales team can actually go see the same people over and over just to make their meeting quota. When you measure first and subsequent, you will quickly see if too much time is spent seeing the same people.

4. **Proposals:** Be careful to only count a proposal on a client need once. Revisions of this proposal should not be counted as additional proposals.

5. **Closes:** You may not consider this an activity, but rather a result. We measure it as activity as the number of closes is a very important statistic to understand how well business is flowing through a salesperson's funnel.

Note: The above activities cover many B2B selling situations but some businesses are unique. One example would be a business that sells at conferences or at trade shows. Here you would measure the number of shows attended and, potentially, the time spent on the floor at shows. Another example would be in the mortgage business where you would measure applications submitted, applications approved and applications funded. The key is to narrow to the critical measures and stay on top of how your team is doing on each.

We have the critical activities, how do we measure and manage them in a One-on-One? The most important numbers in our view are meetings and proposals. Why? Both are "hard" numbers. I can look at your calendar and see the meetings. I can review your proposals. We would call prospecting a "soft" number. Our sales team enters all prospecting reach-outs in our Customer Relationship Management (CRM) but it is one where salespeople might just "dial for dollars" very quickly with no research and no effectiveness to ensure they hit their number. I am not suggesting they are being deceptive, they are goal driven and if we say 200 reach-outs in a month, they will get there. If I put all my focus on that number, they will achieve it but it will not necessarily improve their performance.

Discuss activity highlights, review planned activities and results and debrief activities. Make notes on the One-on-One form.

We are moving through the agenda for a world-class One-on-One. The last two items on the agenda — the action plan (what employee agrees/plans to do) and help needed (what manager agrees/plans to do) — are not actually left until the end of the One-on-One. They are filled in during the meeting, but it is important to review these items at the end of the meeting.

5. Help Needed

This section of the One-on-One form is to keep track of the commitments you make to help the salesperson. Be careful, sales leaders often take on too many tasks. Ask yourself, "Do they really need me to do this or could they do it themselves?" Enable them and save yourself creating an expectation that you may not have time for or may not accomplish.

SALES MANAGER DOING SALESPERSON'S TO-DO LIST

We were hired by one of the most respected brands in the world to help their inside sales managers who coached the telephone sales team. Before designing training I sat in on a One-on-One session. They had 30-minute One-on-Ones every other week with each of their salespeople. The One-on-One was very good with one exception.

At the end, the sales manager had 7 items on his action plan. He had 12 people who reported to him. We did the math, 12 people x 7 items x twice per month. That's 168 things to do every month. Ouch! We then reviewed the list of seven and found only two that he needed to do. Five could have been taken on by the salesperson. He was trying to be helpful and in the process overloading himself and taking away tasks that could help his team develop.

The One-on-One form will help you. The box for your action plan is smaller than the box for the salesperson's action plan.

Commitments you make should be noted and you must hold yourself accountable for completing the task. If you do not keep your commitments, neither will your salesperson.

6. Action Plan

During the meeting, any actions the salesperson commits to should be noted. *At the end of the One-on-One have the salesperson repeat their commitments.* Make sure they know the action plan and that they are committed to its completion. Let them know that you will review the action plan at your next meeting and review with them the support you committed to, to show them that you are accountable too.

Sales Manager Preparation

Preparation is key. It builds confidence and improves competence in your One-on-Ones. The benefits are many when you prepare to meet with your salespeople.

- Maximizes the effectiveness of the conversation.
- Models the preparation you want salespeople to do for their key client meetings.
- Gets you in the right headspace.

- Advances the conversation (alternative is a repeat of previous conversations).

We expect our salespeople to prepare before meetings. If they do not prepare for calls/meetings we go on with them, we are disappointed or upset. Salespeople have the same expectation of us! If we do not prepare for our meetings with them, they see it as a signal that it is okay to not prepare for calls/meetings.

Preparing for a One-on-One is critical. Successful coaches begin visualizing the desired outcome and planning questions to support that outcome before the meeting. As experienced sales managers, we need to ensure we stay disciplined around preparation.

Your One-on-One preparation has six steps. This preparation should not take more than 5 to 10 minutes if you have your file in place.

1. Review the last few meetings. Using your file folder (more on this in the next section) you can easily look at your last few One-on-Ones. If you are using the form it is easy to spot key messages and key actions agreed to.

2. Review their activity, their pipeline and their results. Use online systems or printed reports.

3. Prepare Big Picture Questions on the One-on-One form and label the 10-point scale.

4. Write two Green Flags on the form.

5. Write two Red Flags on the form.

6. Write quick notes to help guide the tactical discussion on Sales Activities and Results.

Manager File for Employee

You know the agenda, you understand the form and how to prepare it, let's make sure we keep a great file of these conversations. Your One-on-One folder for each salesperson should contain the following:

- goals for the month, quarter, year and
- sales or territory plan.

You should prepare using the standard One-on-One form and use this form during the One-on-One to write additional notes. Reviewing meetings from past months will then take only a few minutes. You will be able to advance the conversation and add value. You will also be able to hold the salesperson accountable to the action plans you help them create.

Want to be a world-class sales manager? Then you need to employ the processes and best practices outlined in the standard agenda and conduct world-class One-on-One meetings following the formula. We know there are many challenges to One-on-Ones, including the following:

- time,
- creating an environment that is open and honest,
- they lose their effectiveness when they are not held regularly or canceled, and
- salespeople only take them seriously if the sales manager demonstrates their importance.

But you'll find there are many benefits to holding regular One-on-One meetings too.

- Clarity and focus for salesperson

- Strong relationship with trust and co-operation
- Identification and removal of barriers to sales team's success
- Salesperson performance to goals
- Increased focus on salesperson's learning, growth and development which leads to engagement!

Make world-class One-on-Ones a high prioirty and you will add value to your efforts as well as your team members'. Great business conversations will build the confidence and skill of your team and keep them engaged. Apply an equally effective discipline to sales meetings and you will motivate and inspire your entire team. World-class One-on-Ones lead to motivating sales meetings and these culminate in a great sales culture. Who knows, one day your salespeople will be heading into One-on-Ones and sales meetings whooping, "Yippee!" Isn't that the goal?

Sales Meetings
that Motivate

THE RESEARCH

2010: Quality of meetings were rated at 6.6 out of 10; weekly meetings were held by 43% of sales managers.

2013: Sales leaders rated their sales meetings on average at 6.3 out of 10; 21% of sales leaders gave themselves an 8 out of 10 or higher, while 79% were $7/10$ or less; over 27% of meetings were rated as $5/10$ or less. In terms of frequency, 82% hold monthly or more frequently with 48% holding weekly meetings.

STRENGTHS

- Sales teams get together and share war stories, brainstorm and they feel they are in it together.
- Leaders feel this gathering makes a sales organization run and work hard to deliver value to their teams.

OPPORTUNITY

- Create value for the team.

- Value comes from skill building. Provide a minimum of one idea/strategy/tactic that will improve their sales game; motivate with some positive reinforcement or reward/recognition.

DEFINITION

- Sales meetings are held weekly, bi-weekly or monthly and bring the team together for 30 to 60 minutes.
- These are distinct from business meetings, strategy sessions or conferences.

FUSION LEARNING POINT OF VIEW

- Sales meetings are a critical component of a great sales culture.
- They must be highly interactive.

GOAL

Sales meetings must receive a minimum rating of 8 out of 10 by the sales team. If the meeting you have planned will not be an 8 or better, our system says cancel and use the time to plan your next few meetings that will be 8+. To achieve 8 out of 10, build the skill of the sales team and motivate them.

Give me an idea and some motivation and I will rate the meeting as an 8 out of 10 or maybe even a 9!

PERSONAL EXPERIENCE –
TEN POUNDS OF STUFF IN
A TWO-POUND BAG

I don't run the sales meetings at Fusion Learning; our sales leader does. As an attendee, for me it is a great meeting when the whole team is engaged. We are challenged to handle a tough objection or brainstorm how to help a stalled sales situation to get moving. I like seeing people put on the spot to demonstrate how to engage a client in a meaningful and deep conversation on their business issue, how they need to see change and what the consequences will be if they do not make that change. Interactivity equals productivity for the team.

One issue that always perplexed me was why sales meetings are so hard to make productive. A former colleague helped me with this definition of a sales meeting (also applies to sales conferences): ten pounds of stuff (you can also use an alternate four letter word that starts with same letter) in a two-pound bag! No wonder it is tough to plan great sales meetings. We try to do too much. Some items we try to put in are:

- best practices,
- motivation,
- education,
- product information,
- company messages,
- goals/expectations,
- skill building,
- team activities,
- fun and
- reward/recognition.

These topics are all important, but the question we need to ask is do they need to be in the sales meeting or is there another way to handle them? Information sharing does not need to be done in person. E-mails, group voice mails, hard copy documents are all great ways to share. Avoid filling the agenda with content that can be equally well served in another way.

Great Sales Meetings

Again, we see that a gathering of the troops — whether one-on-one, as in the previous chapter, or the whole gang as in sales meetings — is recognized as important and part of the sales culture. What we need to do is make them a not-to-be-missed component of a great sales culture that builds the engagement of our team.

Typically traditional Sales Meetings are regarded as:

- sales leader dominated (70% of talk time),
- result focused (we are X% short of our target),
- information based,
- individuals on team share in detail what they did last week or will do this week and
- a necessary evil.

At Fusion Learning we strive for excellent Sales Meetings. There are many traits to a Fusion Sales Meeting.

- Team contributes and shares (leader speaks 30% maximum)
- Activity and result focused
- Skill based
- Individuals practice and solve more than share

- Essential component to team success

Manager preparation before meeting on a standard form (see Figure 6) is vital.

If our goal is to have all Sales Meetings rank at 8 out of 10, we need to find a formula to put into place and follow. As we've seen, consistency leads to results. It will need to be a lot of things to a lot of people — always a challenge — but we're up to the challenge, right?

Keys to Excellent Sales Meetings

Let's go back to our research at the top of this chapter and do a little projecting. If you combine the frequency of sales meetings with their quality, the crux of the issue with sales meetings can be illustrated. Imagine a sales leader who holds weekly sales meetings for 45 minutes with a 10-member sales team and rates the meetings as 6 out of 10. (This would be the average sales leader from our sales culture survey.) The sales productivity time on these meetings would be 375 hours annually (45 minutes x 50 weeks x 10 people). One sales team could have 375 hours of productive time that nets them a return that they rate as 6 out of 10. Ouch!

At Fusion Learning we've developed six keys to a successful team meeting.

1. Start with an Energizer
2. Keep It Simply Simple (K.I.S.S.)
3. Three Rules for Individual Updates
4. Motivate and Reward
5. Capability Activity

The final component is to use a standard agenda (see Figure 6). These standard forms keep us focused and on track. So if we are going to start with an energizer, let's get going.

Figure 6: **Sales Meeting Agenda**

SALES MEETING FORM

MODULE	DURATION	START TIME	CATEGORY	ACTIVITY	ACTIVITY EXPLANATION
Open/Energizer	5 minutes	8:30 AM	Company	Image Of	Bring a series of images (for example: a gold medal, a weight lifter, a rocket ship, a race car, etc.). Each team member has to pick one that they feel best represents the work environment or the company's goals and explain why to the large group.
Capability Activity	20 minutes	8:35 AM	Prospecting	Objection Drills	Ask all team members to come to the meeting with the biggest or most common objections they hear when prospecting. As a team, develop options on how to manage, diffuse or break through the objections.
Team/Business Update	15 minutes	8:55 AM	Mid-Month Meeting	Revenue Progress	Share progress on revenue results and discuss how to maintain or dial up as a team and individually.
Individual Update	15 minutes	9:10 AM	Closed Business	Focus	Ask team members to share one thing they will focus on in an upcoming deal that they believe will help them close the business faster.
Other	0 minutes	9:25 AM			
Reward and Recognize	5 minutes	9:25 AM	Team Recognition	Growth within existing accounts	Starbucks Gift Card
Total Meeting Time	60 minutes				

© 2014 Fusion Learning Inc.

Key #1: Start with an Energizer

Salespeople are high energy and it is important that we tap into this energy early and often in a sales meeting. Start all meetings on time and start with some fun. Get the team involved and reward those who show up on time — you will be amazed that if you start every meeting with some fun the lateness factor will go away.

There are six categories for sales meeting energizers. Here they are with three sample energizers for each category. (At Fusion Learning we have a performance support tool for sales meetings that has 70 energizers for sales managers.)

1. **Fun**

   • **Video Clip:** Look up this week's most popular You-Tube videos and share them with the team for a good laugh.

   • **Adjective Name Game:** Ask each team member to choose an adjective that begins with the first letter of their name. It has to be one that suits their personality.

   • **Smarties Trivia:** Pass around a bag of Smarties and tell individuals that they can take as many as they want. Once everyone has some Smarties, let them know that they have to say one thing about themselves for each Smartie that they took.

2. **Business**

   • **In the News:** Prior to the meeting, send the team a business article you pulled from the Internet or the newspaper. Ask them to come prepared to share what they have learned from the article. At the meeting, ask volunteers to share insights from the article and how they will use it in their selling efforts.

- **Word of the Week:** Ask people to pick one word that would represent business success. Put all the words on a flipchart. Everyone gets one vote. Whichever word gets the most votes is the one you use throughout the meeting and the week to drive success and build energy.

- **Stand Up Favorites:** Everyone stands up and shares their perspective on a question. For example, ask, "What's most important for this team this week?" or "How do we want our customers viewing our business?"

3. Sales

- **Sales Highlight:** Everyone shares their sales highlight from last week and explains why it's the highlight.

- **Sales Tips:** Each team member shares something they learned about great salesmanship "way back when" and who they learned it from.

- **Image of:** Bring a series of images (for example, a gold medal, a weight lifter, a rocket ship, a race car, etc.). Each team member has to pick one that best represents their role or their focus in sales for the upcoming quarter and be prepared to share how this ties in with their goals.

4. Personal

- **Twenty Questions:** Prior to the meeting, create a list of 20 or more questions. Ask a team member to pick a number and read the corresponding question on the list. Ask them to answer. Some examples are: What activities did you do in high school? What was your first pet's name? If you were not in this profession, what would you be doing? If you could have lunch with anyone, who would it be? What's in the backseat of your car? What's your favorite thing to wear?

- **If I Were:** Create a deck of question cards. Have team members pull two cards and choose one of the questions to answer. Some question examples are: If I were a kitchen utensil, I would be _____ and explain why; If I were a pizza topping, I would be _____ and explain why.

- **Yesterday, Today, Tomorrow:** Hand each team member a blank piece of 8½ x 11 paper. Ask them to fold it evenly in three. On the top fold have them draw a picture that symbolizes where they were 5 years ago, in the middle have them draw something that symbolizes where they are today and on the last fold tell them to draw who or where they hope to be in 5 years. Have participants share with the large group.

5. Company

- **Fascinating People:** Give your team 20 to 30 seconds to think of someone outside of their team who they feel brings value to the company and share it with the large group.

- **Values:** Ask each team member to share a 1-minute story where the company's values were demonstrated recently.

- **Company Fun:** Each team member shares, in 1 minute or less, a fun story that happened in the office or with clients.

6. **Strategy**

   - **Focus:** Ask each team member to share one area of focus for the month ahead that will help them meet their quarterly goals.

   - **Flags:** On different colored Post-its, each team member shares one thing the whole group is really good at and one thing the whole team needs to get better at to reach targets. Have the team plan ideas for improvement on the "get better" list.

   - **Pictionary:** Each team member is given a blank piece of paper and a pen. Ask each to draw a "visual representation or image" of the team's goals.

The topics are meant to give you variety in your sales meetings. Some topics are related to the business, some are related to team building and some are to lighten up the team with some fun.

WHOOPEE!

One of my fellow shareholders at Fusion Learning used to lead our sales team. He followed our formula, so one Monday we all came to the meeting and he announced that the energizer would consist of him giving each of us one Post-it note. He preceded to hand to the five of us one each and then announced that the energizer portion of the sales meeting was complete.

We all looked at him inquisitively. He shared that the Post-it was going to be our vote for the best participant at the meeting. He would hold the vote at the end of the meeting with the winner taking home the prize, which was a nice crisp wine bag at the front of the room. We were energized and when the energy slipped a few times in the meeting, he waved the voting cards and got us going.

I clearly remember this meeting as I took the vote for best participant and was handed the wine bag, which turned out to be very light as it did not hold a bottle of wine but instead a whoopee cushion. Bummer (chuckle, chuckle), but it did come in very handy at our next sales meeting when one of our team was describing how she planned to close multiple deals that week. Whoopee!

Use variety in energizers and keep them simple, which is a great lead-in to the next key to successful sales meetings.

Key #2: Keep It Simply Simple (K.I.S.S.)

A list of potential topics for a sales meeting shows you it is easy to complicate the meeting. Try to put 10 pounds of … stuff in a two-pound bag and we all know what happens. Keep your sales meeting agenda lean and mean. Always ask, "Does this item need to be in the meeting or could it be done outside the meeting or as pre-work?"

TO STRUT OR TO SUCCEED?

Years ago I worked with one of the world's most successful mutual fund firms. It was in the 90s and at the time mutual funds were the hot commodity. This firm was bringing in $2 or $3 billion in new investment weekly. With new investment come new funds. The marketing team was launching a new fund every month.

The hundreds of associates who were on the phones servicing investors and advisors needed to learn the funds. The only issue — the phone associates were too busy servicing clients to fit learning into their schedules. So, the marketing team paid them overtime to come in at 7 or 8 am, before their shift, to "learn" about the new fund. I put "learn" in quotation marks because as the associates came in, the marketing team pulled out a beautiful PowerPoint, dimmed the lights and told them everything they needed to know. Perfect other than the majority of the associates used the time to catch up on their sleep.

We were tasked to help improve the process. Our solution was to send the PowerPoint as a pre-read and then hold a competition with prizes. Associates would volunteer to come up in front of the group and take a mock call from a client who would be played by the marketing team. The client would ask questions about the fund. After the mock call the marketing team would lead feedback on the call and correct any facts not delivered correctly. Associates would be motivated to do the pre-study during slow call times as they would have a chance to strut their stuff at the fund launch and they would receive a prize for volunteering.

Great solution that unfortunately the marketing team turned down. They had worked damn hard for months to create a new fund and much as they wanted (needed) the associates to learn, they wanted the chance to strut their stuff in front of their superiors who attended the sessions.

The proposed solution followed the second principle of sales meetings — K.I.S.S. Send information in advance that people can study. Create a fun, interactive exercise to actually apply the information rather than to share it and allow people to practice the use of the information rather than to simply be told it.

Great, so how do we keep it simply simple? Just four steps.

1. Fast
2. Fun
3. Create Value
4. Shared Ownership

Fast

The pace of a sales meeting should match the pace you want the team to work at. So if it is early Monday, starting with 10 minutes of people sharing what they did on the weekend is setting a bad pace and encouraging us to take it easy in selling this week. The meeting is scheduled for 8 am on Monday and at 8 am on the dot the sales leader begins the energizer that sets a great pace and takes 5 minutes. Those who are late miss out and walk into a room that is alight with energy. We all know people are creatures of habit and if that is how each meeting starts, who wants to miss the beginning?

10:29:45 AM

My first year university professor for business was Frank Mastrandrea. Frank had 90 19-year-olds who came to his class at 10:30 am. He had exactly 50 minutes with us to cover one case study from analysis to recommendations to implementation. A tough task to say the least.

For the entire school year, Frank stood at the front of the class and chatted with us as we entered the room. At 10:29 and 45 seconds, Frank assumed his spot at the very front and stared at the clock that was mounted at the rear of the room for 15 seconds. At precisely 10:30 am, Frank began the class with a hearty welcome and he immediately got us working energetically.

Within a few weeks of the start of the year it was abundantly clear to all that class started at 10:30 sharp and guess what? We were all there in our seats without ever being told. Nice!

So, start on time and set a great pace. Check your pace regularly with the team. If you feel energy slipping, stop what you are doing and move to the next item on your agenda. Remember that your tone of voice, the pitch, the enunciation, the volume all need to be different in a group setting than when you are One-on-One. Dramatically different. Check yourself — if you are using similar pace and energy in the team setting as when you are one on one, make some changes!

Fun

Who does not love to laugh, to embellish, to kid, to cajole and to banter? And don't salespeople love all of these? How do you create an atmosphere that brings these characteristics to your meeting? I am not suggesting you have to bring them all; you have to set the tone that allows them. Fun and laughter are keys to getting them to come back, to enjoy and to appreciate the team time. There will be times when we may need to be more serious — when we are in tough economic times or well behind plan — but some fun is always welcome.

APRIL FOOL

The Fusion Learning team loves to have fun. One day in April I am in my office and David comes to tell me that Natalia, assistant to our landlord (they are on the floor above us) is here and needs to see me.

Natalia (Nat for short) comes in and explains to me that they have put in some added security cameras and there is some footage that she needs to show me — some disturbing footage. Taking the bait, I start to inquire. Is it outside? "No, it is in your space. In fact, it's in your office."

"Well, what is it?"

Nat replies, "Best I show you. I don't really want to describe it."

"OK," I say. Nat gets up and says follow me. We proceed to our kitchen where the whole Fusion Learning team is waiting. I pull Nat aside (still not getting it — duh!). "Should we not look at it in private?"

"No," she says. "We are okay." The video then rolls and it is a video that the team has taken of what they do in my office when I am away for the day. Team members are drinking, stealing items, checking my files, using my stuff, having a party, dancing and a few things that are not fit to publish. It was a hilarious video, a great spoof on the boss and a fun way to celebrate — you guessed it — April Fool's Day.

Don't expect fun to happen — create it and welcome it.

Create Value

The goal is 8 out of 10 as rated by the team. You are not getting that score if you have not helped them to close more business. There are six areas to create value.

1. Prospecting
2. Networking
3. Lead Generation
4. Client Meetings/Learning Client Needs
5. Presenting Solutions
6. Closing

In creating value you need to help salespeople with how to better execute one of these tasks. A bit later in the chapter we'll discuss more precise ways for how to engage the team in learning in these six areas.

Shared Ownership

Get team members to present and share content on a regular basis. Don't abdicate to them — they may show up and deliver well below the 8 out of 10. Delegate to them and ask that they give you a briefing prior to the meeting. You are keeping it simple for you and you will need to help them to keep it simple, relevant and impactful. Benefits to sharing the agenda are buy-in, participation and energy for the team as they see different people and styles.

Awesome — our sales meeting is going great, a solid 8.5 out of 10 and I come to the third item on my agenda — individual updates from each member of the team.

Key #3: Individual Updates

"Let's all share what happened in our territory last week."

First team member gives a short and snappy summary. Same for the second. Then Joe, our 23-year veteran, gets his turn and wouldn't you know he can take a short story and make it long. Team meeting slides to 7.5, no 6.5, and 3 minutes later he has opened a few large issues and riled up the team. How did things go so wrong so quickly?

Individual updates are fantastic and a very important part of team meetings with one caveat: the topic must be small, the answers must be timed and you must manage it so that they add value as opposed to sapping energy.

So, three simple rules for individual updates.

1. Set time limits!
2. Create different themes:
   - Successes
   - Key Learnings
   - Focus for time ahead
3. Know when to take individual issues offline.

Time Limits

Setting time limits is pretty obvious. The most important factor is to be explicit on the time allowed.

- "You have 30 seconds."

- "We have a total of 10 minutes so if the person before you leaves time, I will add to yours but if they go over, I will subtract."

- "One minute per person with the best answer in the shortest time getting a loonie (that's a Canadian dollar)."

- Pull out your watch, allow everyone to see and be sure to stop the first person who hits the time limit. When you do this, most people will use much less than the allowed time as no one wants to be seen as not following the rules.

Buzzzzzz, time's up!

Themed Updates

I love updates in meetings. Assigning a theme to the updates engages members' brains and often makes a great segue into Key #4 — Reward!

Here are some of my favorite questions to ask.

1. Describe a proud sales moment from last week.

2. Tell us a problem you faced last week and what you did to solve it.

3. Who was your favorite client last week and why?

4. Share an objection you faced and how you handled it.

5. What was the toughest question you were asked by a client and that you asked a client last week?

6. Share two actions you took that saved you time.

7. Detail in one sentence your weeks' activities.

8. Identify one of your teammates that you saw being highly productive last week and what they were doing that gave you that impression.

9. What behavior of yours from last week will you change this week and why?

10. Which day last week was your best and why?

11. Share one client situation you will move forward this week and how.

12. List three clients you must reach this week and what you will do to achieve this.

13. What are your three most important tasks this week?

14. Picture Friday at 4 pm. What have you accomplished that made it a fantastic week?

15. In an ideal world, clients would call us back immediately. Who do you want to call you this week and how will you make it happen?

16. List your top five things to do for the week.

17. Who is one member of the team you could help this week and share your plan to do it?

18. What will be your toughest challenge this week and what help do you need?

19. Pick an important client meeting this week. What will the client be saying after it and what do you have left to do to guarantee that outcome?

20. Name one thing you will do this week to bring fun to you and the team.

Offline Individual Issues

Managing an interactive sales meeting can be a bit tricky to keep on target at first. Do not allow "issues" to derail (people love to complain, and this is the time it might come out). If needed, take it offline. Keep these points in mind.

- Maintain the team's focus. If a question is not answered, say you will come back to them (and be sure you do).
- Set the pace by going first and give a great answer with time to spare.

Done right, individual updates can be a highlight in meetings and done wrong they are the number one killer of a great meeting. But getting to the Motivate and Reward segment of any sales meeting is the climax!

Key #4: Motivate and Reward

Motivation is a critical component to any team meeting and must be built in. The team has a tough challenge and they want to feel supported and recognized for their hard work. It is not about big gifts or exceptional moments; it is the simplest of thank yous that have great meaning.

Think about sorting the rewards into different categories.

1. Fun Awards

- I had one client who annually gave away the "green jacket" to the top salesperson. The fun thing about it was that it was not a beautiful green jacket. It was the most god-awful ugly jacket that no one would wear in public — but if you were lucky enough to receive it, you would wear it often in the halls at work.

- The Fusion Learning sales team awards the Buddha for salesperson of the month — and the honor comes with the right to house the wooden Buddha in your office for the month. (We used to have an ugly yellow Buddha that was replaced with the new and improved philosopher.)

- Best sales line of the week award, with weekly quotes being captured so you can award the annual best award.

FUN DONE WRONG

Years ago, early in my sales career, I was accompanied by my manager on a client meeting. During the meeting I used a metaphor about an elephant which he did not like. He took over the conversation and, after the meeting, without asking my opinion, let me know that it was a poor metaphor. To this day I still feel strongly it was appropriate.

To add insult to injury, at out next team meeting, in recognition of me signing business with the client from that meeting, he presented me with a plaque recognizing "Best Use of an Elephant Metaphor in a Client Meeting." I still have the plaque and it is a constant reminder that fun awards can be done wrong — be careful!

2. Competitive Awards

- Create mini-competitions among the team around goals or key metrics.

- Divide the team into sub-teams and have them help each other to achieve a goal around calls made or meetings booked or proposals issued.

- Send pre-work in advance of the meeting and have each team member demonstrate a sales practice or pitch with the team voting on the best demonstration.

3. Team Awards

- Team-related incentive around a goal or key metric.

- Draw team names from a hat (return your own name if you pull it) and then have each person recognize the team member they pulled for support they have provided to them.

4. Recognition Awards

- High achievement

- Over plan performance

- Highest activity

- Strongest customer satisfaction

5. External Awards

- Get feedback from outside on team or individual performance.

- Non-sales team to give recognition to sales team.

- Sales team recognition of those outside the team who support them.

Every sales meeting should have some recognition, from a simple thank you to each team member to a more formal monthly or yearly program.

Key #5: Capability Activity

Give a man a fish and you feed him for a day.
Teach a man to fish and you feed him for a lifetime.
— *Chinese Proverb*

Salespeople are professionals. Like any professional, be they lawyer or teacher or therapist, you must have ongoing professional development to stay at the top of your game. Every sales meeting must stretch and challenge team members' skills and expertise. It is the key to creating value and delivering on the expectation of your sales team giving you at least an 8 out of 10. Here are some ideas.

1. Prospecting

- **Objection Drills:** Ask all team members to come to the meeting with the biggest or most common objections they hear when prospecting. As a team, develop options on how to manage, diffuse or break through the objections.

- **Prospecting Role Plays:** Have team members bring in three calls they plan to make that day. In pairs, ask team members to practice their calls back to back. Fishbowl (role play in front of the whole group) two examples and have the rest of the group provide feedback.

2. Networking

- **Social Media Best Practice:** Have team members share best practices in leveraging social media (like LinkedIn) for networking.

- **Follow Up:** Have team craft follow-up letters, e-mails and phone calls to individuals they met at a networking event.

3. Lead Generation

- **Lead Source Brainstorm:** As a team, think about your top five customers in the past six months. For each of the customers, identify where the lead came from. Brainstorm ways to leverage similar lead sources moving forward.

- **Centers of Influence:** Have the team discuss and determine five centers of influence for your business. Fashion ways the team could leverage these centers of influence in order to generate new leads.

4. Client Meetings

- **Two-One-Two Brainstorm:** Prior to the meeting, ask team members to think about an upcoming client meeting that they need some help with. At the meeting, ask for a volunteer to share the background of their situation (give them 2 minutes). The rest of the team then has 1 minute to ask questions about it. The team then has 2 minutes to share different ideas for the meeting.

- **Opening:** Have team members be ready to share how they plan to open five upcoming meetings, along with two Thoughtful Questions they will use in the meetings. The team provides feedback and suggestions.

5. Presenting Solutions

- **Benefit Statements:** List the features of one of your solutions. As a team, create statements for each feature that focuses on the benefit to the customer versus the feature of the solution itself.

- **Success Stories:** Ask each team member to share a success story on how they presented a solution. As a group, determine what elements triggered the success.

6. Closing

- **Closing Practice:** Ask team members to bring information on an upcoming close to the meeting. Have team members role play the close in front of the group (team member chooses someone to play the role of their customer). Provide feedback to improve their closing skills.

- **Buying Signals:** As a team, review the most common buying signals that should trigger us to ask for the business. What do our clients say or do when they are ready to move ahead? How will we respond?

Key #6: Standard Agenda

While this is not part of an excellent sales meeting, it will help you to create them and ensure that you continue to rank 8 out of 10 or better. Keep the agendas in a folder so you don't repeat any of the fun and creative segments. Fusion Learning has a performance support tool that automates the process and contains everything needed to create hundreds of great sales meetings.

As a sales manager, you likely started out as a sales person. While you were great at building the relationship with clients, actually managing people may have been a bit of a challenge. So these last three disciplines have likely given you a number of new ideas to implement to take you to the next level of management and to be successful at engaging your sales team. As we approach pipeline management you see it as one of your strengths. This is right up your alley. But hold on a minute. There may be more to this than closing the deal.

CHAPTER

7

Are You a Deal Manager or a Sales Manager (Pipeline Management)?

THE RESEARCH

The Question: "Pipeline helps drive sales productivity in our sales organization?"

The Response 2006: 4.7 out of 10.

The Response 2010: 6.3 out of 10.

The Response 2013: 6.7 out of 10.

The Question: "We have an easy-to-follow process for keeping sales pipeline/funnel up to date."

The Response: 67% said yes; 33% said no.

STRENGTHS

- CRM systems have helped sales organizations to create more detailed, easier-to-read, easier-to-update and, most importantly, easier-to-interpret sales pipelines.

- Sales leaders are often deal managers despite the advances in technology that can allow them to be both deal and pipeline managers.
- Salespeople pay attention to important deals in play and often are unaware of the overall health of their pipeline.
- With a poor pipeline the emphasis on deals in play will increase, as with few deals available, quota achievement relies on a high close rate.

DEFINITION

- The heart of pipeline management is a pipeline review, a quick (15 minutes or less), tactical, scheduled meeting between a manager and a salesperson held once per week or every other week.
- Pipelines: Healthy, False Hope, Thin and Congested.

FUSION LEARNING POINT OF VIEW

- Pipeline management must be frequent, tactical, quick and reality based. It includes deal management and the overall shape of the pipeline.

GOAL

Salesperson and sales leader are always in alignment on the type of pipeline a salesperson has and the activity required in moving it to, or keeping it at, Healthy.

When the pipeline is poor, emphasis must be placed on adding opportunities, in addition to helping with the deals in play!

PERSONAL EXPERIENCE – NOT WHERE I NEED IT TO BE!

Seventy-five percent of salespeople do not have a healthy pipeline. When they are asked to diagnose the shape of their pipeline they can give an honest assessment. They know if it is healthy and they know if it is not. They do not and their sales leaders do not need a report to tell them. The shape of the pipeline shows up every day in their activity and in their emotions.

Definitions to Set the Stage

Just to get us all on the same page, let's distinguish between a deal manager and a sales manager and what their roles are within pipeline coaching and revenue goals.

- **The Deal Manager:** Usually, this type of sales leader proves to be a great salesperson, and because of this is promoted to manager. He or she is an excellent closer, loves to discuss the hot deals, is very good at strategizing a customer situation and, if the numbers come up a little short for the quarter, month or year, will do what it takes to hit the targets.

- **The Sales Manager:** In most cases, this sales leader concentrates on developing the skills and abilities of the team, realizing that this will allow the team's leader to be successful as well. The sales manager believes that the sales manager's job is, not to create sales, but to create salespeople.

If we look at a couple of critical sales management tactics from both perspectives, we see the strength or frailty in each one. Of course, the best of both worlds would be a sales manager who can also be a deal manager when the need arises.

MANAGE THE DEAL OR MANAGE THE PEOPLE?

Back in my early sales career, my first sales manager was a deal manager. He coached me on any opportunity that was in front of me and helped me to strategize how to win. He pushed me if I was behind and recognized me when I brought in a sizable deal. He was not aware that I was unhappy and looking at other opportunities. He was fortunate because I did not find the greener pasture on his watch. If I had I would not have hesitated to resign.

My second sales manager paid attention to me. He quickly realized I was not loving my role and committed to help me become happier or move to a different role. The process took 6 months and guess what? My sales results were excellent during this time. He was managing me, and he was managing my deals — I was motivated to do my best as he helped me to be my best.

Pipeline Coaching

As a *deal manager*, you are really interested in two things: the deals that are closest to closing and the big deals. You love to engage in conversations about them — what is happening in the sales process, explore what else you can do and how you can help.

As a *sales manager*, you want to know the overall health of your sales team's pipeline. If it is healthy, the team will have enough customer situations and deal volume to sustain them for the next quarter and beyond. Then your task is to help with deal management. If your salespeople's pipelines are not healthy (about 75% of all sales pipelines), then you need to talk about the steps they are taking to grow their pipelines. This coaching will help you and the team long term.

The Caution: You can see the pitfall of deal management in pipeline coaching. Deal managers will do everything to help their salespeople close what is in their sights, and they might miss the big picture, which is that their salespeople do not have enough deals in the pipeline for the future.

Revenue Goals

The sales organization must deliver on revenue commitments to the company. As a *deal manager*, if your annual target is $10 million, you can bet that you will help close everything needed and deliver the number.

As a *sales manager*, you will pay attention to your revenue number and participation rate — the percent of your team that is at or above plan. You know that you have to have at least 70% participation if you want to make plan, and you will most likely overachieve. You also know that if 70% of your people make plan, they will stay, and your job next year will get easier.

The Caution: Deal managers might ride the High Performers to help crest the goal, and in this action, they and their salespeople suffer from burnout. This can lead to the first-quarter hangover, when they experience really low sales while they try to recover.

Participation rate is a metric that is often not formally measured in sales organizations. Sales leaders are measured by hitting their revenue number, not by every person on their team having to hit their number. Even a Poor Performer who is at 40% of their quota is making a contribution to the sales leader's numbers. If they are cut from the team, the team's left with an open territory and some lost sales. If sales leaders are measured by revenue and participation rate, low performers need to be helped up or out. Sales leaders will also make the decision as to what to do with these low performers sooner; the sooner the decision is made, the sooner the participation rate can be improved. One way to look at participation rate is to think of the bell curve. Sales teams typically have a few stars, lots of middle performers and a few who are not currently successful — the bell curve of performance. Participation rate causes sales leaders to shift the curve up, get more people into the high performance category (curve shifts to the right), and make quicker decisions on Poor Performers (remove the tail from the curve).

Pipeline Management System

In order to discuss pipelines let's start with the acknowledgement that each organization has its unique characteristics and words that are used to label pipeline. Some call it pipeline, some call it funnel. No matter what the words, a pipeline includes all opportunities that may turn into a sale now or in the future.

There are three parts to any pipeline. The development of these parts within the pipeline defines the type of pipeline; there are four of these. The qualities of the salespeople who manage each of these four types of pipelines will provide different challenges to sales managers.

The Pipeline Parts

In our words, there are three stages to a funnel or pipeline.

1. Prospects
2. Opportunities
3. Closes

A *prospect* is a situation that is not fully sighted but where we believe we will have an opportunity in the future (before becoming a prospect we just had suspects beyond the pipeline). It might be that we know they have a need, or a budget. We are unclear exactly what or when but we suspect that business will happen in the future.

An *opportunity* is a situation that is identified. Typically we have identified BANT: Budget, Authority, Need and Timeline. It is now sighted so it is an opportunity.

Closes are when we sign the business. In essence this is a moment in time when it moves from opportunity to close by way of an approval (signature) but in considering pipeline it is critical to pay attention to the number and dollar volume of closes as they are critical to diagnosing pipeline health. Consistent quantity and volume of closes on a month-by-month basis indicates a healthy pipeline.

The evolution of pipeline (in our words) is when suspects (above the pipeline) become prospects who then become opportunities and then they close or — they are removed from the pipeline at some point during the sales process when it is clear they will not lead to a sale. The distribution of prospects, opportunities and closes defines the type of pipeline. In working with hundreds of sales organizations we recognize this is a simplistic view of the funnel and in your organization it might have four or five stages.

Types of Pipelines

At the core of pipeline management are four types of pipelines (see Figure 7.1):

1. **Healthy:** A healthy funnel has lots of prospects or opportunities at the start of the sales cycle. It has lots of opportunities (with a healthy undiscounted dollar volume) and it is consistently delivering sales each month (or each period that is realistic to deliver sales).

2. **False Hope:** A false hope pipeline has lots of prospects, lots of opportunities and yet it does not deliver closes. Everything seems strong but each month seems to end with excuses instead of deals. Typically the false hope is in the opportunities, not the prospects. Often there are opportunities that should be removed as they are no longer active or realistic to close. Some salespeople like to keep everything on the pipeline as that is their reminder to stay in touch.

3. **Thin:** A thin pipeline has a few prospects, a few opportunities and it has infrequent closes. The good news is that the salesperson can move a suspect to prospect to an opportunity and then to close. The bad news is that the volume in all stages of the pipeline is not nearly enough.

Figure 7.1: **Types of Sales Pipelines**

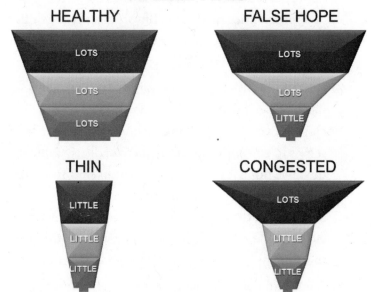
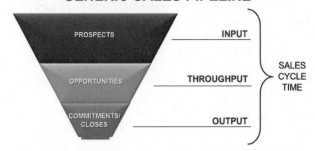

SALES PIPELINE TYPES

GENERIC SALES PIPELINE

PROSPECTS — INPUT

OPPORTUNITIES — THROUGHPUT

COMMITMENTS/CLOSES — OUTPUT

SALES CYCLE TIME

PIPELINE TYPES

HEALTHY
LOTS
LOTS
LOTS

FALSE HOPE
LOTS
LOTS
LITTLE

THIN
LITTLE
LITTLE
LITTLE

CONGESTED
LOTS
LITTLE
LITTLE

© 2014 Fusion Learning Inc.

4. **Congested:** A congested pipeline has lots and lots of prospects but few turn into opportunities and thus very few closes. Healthy top of the pipeline but the rest is congested.

As one might expect the types of salespeople who manage these four types of pipelines will differ.

Match the Salesperson to the Pipeline

A salesperson with a Healthy funnel is a busy person. They are active. They are on the phone. They are hustling. You will not find them at the water cooler socializing. The time of the month is not relevant to them as they are not time driven; they are customer focused and they know how to balance prospecting with opportunity management with deal closing.

Those with False Hope funnels struggle to truly understand what is a deal and what is not. They will spend a lot of time on a deal and when they take along their manager or a more seasoned salesperson, that person can "smell" that there is not a deal. They will not hear from or be in communication with a client who is on their pipeline as their calls/e-mails are not being returned and yet they will still talk about the deal as coming soon. The average time on pipeline for their situations will be much higher than team and industry norms. The volume on the pipeline may look healthy but the monthly closes are far from being on pace. When asked what will close this month, the list is a wish list not a realistic, fact-based summary. When the month passes with no or few closes, they are surprised (others are not).

CLEARING THE FALSE HOPE

Many sales organizations have an issue with False Hope pipelines because their sales team wants to keep all potential deals on their list so they don't forget to stay in touch. We encountered this at Fusion Learning when, at one point, we pushed our sales team to clean up the pipeline.

We found many deals in different salespeople's funnels that they classified as not active but they did not want to remove. These were delayed or postponed deals and they wanted to keep them in focus despite no timetable for when they may be revived.

We reached a compromise by creating a category called "stalled" with an estimated chance of closing set at 0%. When we run a pipeline report we do not include stalled opportunities on it. If a salesperson wants to view all potential deals, they can run the report and choose to include stalled. What had been False Hope (including the Stalled) suddenly became thin or congested.

The Thin pipeline salesperson might be presumed to be not very busy. This can be the case but is not always so. They are often busy being busy. They will ensure every "i" is dotted and every "t" is crossed. Their paperwork is perfect. They know how to move a deal through the funnel and can do it effectively but not efficiently. They have a tendency to create the perfect proposal, but not manage the time they put into it. Every task is a priority with one big exception — prospecting to add more to the funnel.

The Congested pipeline salesperson is a great hunter. They have no call reluctance and are active on the phone and working their network. They meet all requirements for call and meeting activity. Their challenge? They do not emerge from first meetings with many opportunities. They are always anxious and excited about upcoming meetings. They will always be ready to talk about who they are seeing tomorrow or next week but when asked after a meeting how it went there is often little to say.

Knowing the four typical pipeline shapes and the salespeople who work them, we can explore how to hold a robust, productive pipeline discussion and move everyone to a Healthy funnel.

Pipeline Review Process

The pipeline review is a tactical and fast meeting to review the pipeline and ensure a clear action plan is in place to move what is on the pipeline and to add to the pipeline.

The flow of the meeting is specific.

1. Big Picture
2. Pipeline Summary
3. New Sales Opportunities
4. Stalled Sales Opportunities
5. Missing Sales Opportunities
6. Closing Sales Opportunities
7. Key Action Items
8. Help Required
9. Anything Else?

In order to prepare for the pipeline review, pull the pipeline report and think about each of the categories. We utilize a standard form (see Figure 7.2) but you do not complete any of it in advance as it will be filled out as you speak to the salesperson.

Figure 7.2: **Sales Pipeline Review Form**

SALES PIPELINE REVIEW FORM

fusion!
LEARNING INC.

Salesperson:

Sales Manager:

Date:

Big Picture:	Key Metric	This Meeting	Last Meeting
1. Funnel Type: ☐ Healthy ☐ False Hope ☐ Thin ☐ Congested			
2. Change from last review? ☐ Yes ☐ No			
3. 0-60 Day Funnel Health? ☐ Poor ☐ OK ☐ Great			
4. 60+ Day Funnel Health: ☐ Poor ☐ OK ☐ Great			
Notes:			

New Sales Opportunities?	Stalled Sales Opportunities?	Missing Sales Opportunities?
1.	1.	1.
2.	2.	2.
3.	3.	3.

Closing Opportunities

Who:	When:

Key Action Items

Item:	Due Date:	Responsible:
1.		
2.		
3.		
4.		
5.		

Help Required?

1.

2.

3.

Notes

© 2014 Fusion Learning Inc.

1. Big Picture

- Ask the salesperson what type of pipeline they currently have — Healthy, False Hope, Thin or Congested and if you agree write it down. If you disagree, question them as to why they feel it is this type. You may need to skip ahead to step two — pipeline summary — to help them to change diagnosis. When you are both in agreement, note the type. As you have the dialogue note any action items in step seven — key action items.

- Ask, "Has this changed since last review?" Note their answer. If it is yes and it has moved to Healthy, congratulate them on their success. This needs to be celebrated so they know Healthy is good! If they have moved out of False Hope to Thin or Congested, also congratulate them on cleaning up their funnel. False Hope has situations on it that should not be there, so when they move to Thin or Congested, help them to know this is the right way to run their business.

- Ask about the short-term pipeline health (for some businesses short term is 30 days, for some it is 90 days and for some it is longer). Is it poor, okay or great? This question dissects the pipeline into two parts — short and long term. You want to recognize up front if you need immediate action to change the pipeline. Again, note action items in step seven. If you agree with their assessment, note it. If you disagree help them through questioning to adjust their point of view. Short-term pipeline health is the most important metric to determine short-term performance by the salesperson.

- Ask about the long-term pipeline health. Is it poor, okay or great? This question is helpful when someone has a Healthy funnel as sometimes it is Healthy for the short term but they are not building the long term. You can use this question to remind them to not neglect prospecting. Those with False Hope, Thin or Congested funnels will most likely have poor long-term health, so you can use this to focus them on prospecting to build the funnel.

2. Pipeline Summary

Create a short simple set of numbers to summarize the quantity on the pipeline. At Fusion Learning, we use four numbers — number of pipeline situations, gross dollar value on the pipeline, net or discounted pipeline value and dollars closed this month. For us a Healthy pipeline has 25 situations worth $1.5 million gross, $900,000 net and closes of $80,000 for the month. In our pipeline review we have two columns, one for this week and one for last review. We copy the four numbers from the last review and then populate the numbers for this review. This quantitative chart shows at a glance how we are progressing (or not). Where you have clear numbers for a Healthy pipeline, always be discussing how the actuals compare to ideal. Note any action items.

The summary section allows a simple view of whether life is moving or we are experiencing *Groundhog Day*.

3. New Sales Opportunities

What has been added to the pipeline since you last met? Celebrate each success — new adds move us closer or keep us at Healthy. At times this might be a blank section. That is all right this week but if it is a common occurrence, not enough work is being done at suspect and prospect level to keep the funnel Healthy.

4. Stalled Sales Opportunities

What seems to be sitting on the pipeline and not moving? Spend time here as this is where you help them decide if it should stay on the pipeline. Let them control what is on and what needs to come off but influence them to remove an entry when it is time so they do not end up with False Hope. In this section and in others, you can easily flip to your last few pipeline reviews to see what has been in this category. Use this data to help remove those that have been discussed on a few occasions as being stalled.

5. Missing Sales Opportunities

Here is where you look for opportunities that they have not put on the pipeline. These could be new opportunities that they have not yet had time to add (you may have already covered these in step three) or opportunities they are not sure are real and they may need help from you to decide whether to add them or not. You may decide to add them or you may not but note the situation here so you have a record of those entries that do not reach the pipeline.

6. Closing Sales Opportunities

You may ask why the deals that are likely to close are item number 6 on the pipeline review. Your energy and the energy of the salesperson will be greatest here — and that is exactly why you wait. If you discuss these up front they have potential to consume you and consume your time. You need to discuss these and at this point you do. You will spend the time required here but in essence you have been strategic on pipeline management for the first 5 to 7 minutes in steps one through five — now you can get tactical on what you need to do to close the opportunities that are most ready from your pipeline. Take your time here. Help the salesperson in any way you can to maximize those sales that need the final push to success.

7. Key Action Items

This list is built as you have the discussion and it is finalized at this point in the conversation. You may have listed action items, but be sure to assign a due date and that responsibility is assigned. Get them to repeat the action plan to ensure they have bought in and are willing to execute in a timely fashion.

8. Help Required

What commitments have you made either to do or support having done? Be careful to ask yourself, "Do I need to do this or could they?" If they can do it, it should be an action item for them not on your list, similar to your action plans in your One-on-Ones.

9. Anything Else?

Recap the pipeline review and congratulate them on any success since you last met. Re-confirm action plans. Encourage them that pipeline changes are possible where effort is extended.

This nine-step process should take about 15 minutes. It may take a little longer if there is a long list of closing situations that need to be discussed and action plans created. One meeting can seem very tactical and may seem like they could mail in the answers — it is the discipline of regular meetings that show the pattern.

Picture four meetings held every two weeks over an eight-week period. In all four, you have a False Hope pipeline that appears to have enough opportunities and none are closing. By the fourth meeting, you will be able to show that a number of situations need to come off the pipeline and your salesperson will now move to Thin or Congested. During these same four meetings you have hopefully helped them to see that long-term pipeline health is poor and have helped them to reinvigorate prospecting so when you move some deadwood off the pipeline, the wheels are already in motion for adding some new situations.

Using technology to help your team members manage their pipelines can be effective, but you and the salesperson must recognize the shape of their funnel first. Then reviewing the pipeline can be quick and authentic. You must do it often and be strategic in your approach. This will move all the pipelines into a healthy state in short order and keep them healthy longer. Healthy Pipelines deliver excellent sales results and when my results are excellent, I am engaged.

Getting out into the field with your salespeople will give even greater insight into their pipelines and will allow you yet another opportunity to coach them.

Field Coaching

THE RESEARCH

The Question: "How productive is the coaching on customer calls?"

The Response 2013: 28% say 8 out of 10 or higher; 20% say 7 out of 10; leaving about one half saying 6 out of 10 or less.

STRENGTHS

- Managers are Field Coaching.
- It is very effective in some companies and in some industries (e.g., the pharmaceutical industry has begun three-way Field Coaching — rep + manager + manager's manager).

OPPORTUNITY

- Frequency and quality can both be improved.
- Veteran reps are the most neglected.
- The quality issue relates to the manager often taking over the sales meeting versus allowing the representative to handle it.

Field Coaching has three key components:

- Before-Meeting coaching,
- During-the-Meeting behavior and coaching and
- After-the-Meeting feedback.

The manager must hold coaching as the priority when it is a coaching call. If it is a closing call, the manager is there for their selling skills; all should be clear that the goal is to get the business.

- Field Coaching must be practiced with all sales team members to increase their skills and confidence.

Excellent coaching prior to the customer meeting that leads to an excellent meeting that leads to a productive feedback session after the call. All sales representatives — new, veteran, experienced, productive, superstars — receive Field Coaching at a minimum of every quarter and, where possible, monthly.

Coach me now or pay me later.

We talk about coach, captain or cheerleader. In Field Coaching, the sales manager often sets out to be coach, but once the customer meeting starts they become captain, doing their best to make sure we score (get the business). Of the hundreds of sales organizations we have worked with at Fusion Learning, it is rare to find companies that are maximizing this coaching opportunity. Tenure seems to preclude the need for coaching, yet the world's best athletes have coaches. During the calls, sales managers see stumbles by the salesperson as the moment to take over the meeting. The need for the deal often wins over the need for learning.

Field Coaching

The coaching skills and Effective Feedback discussed in Part II are used in Field Coaching but the process has a specific structure. I tend to say "pay me now or pay me later" in Field Coaching with two meanings.

- If you coach your salesperson before the call you will avoid having a lot of coaching after the meeting with an added benefit of a much improved call.

- If you constantly take over the meeting from your salesperson you may win deals but you will not develop your team member.

Field Coaching takes place in three settings:

- Before-Meeting coaching,

- During-the-Meeting behaviour and coaching and
- After-the-Meeting feedback.

All three components require structure and discipline.

Before-Meeting Coaching

Our goal is to set our salesperson up for success. In order to do this we must help them with their skills and with their confidence. Keep to the coaching and cheerleading role here. You don't want to become the captain and provide the plays. Let the salesperson do the work while you provide the support and encouragement from the sidelines.

Be careful that this step is completed well in advance of the client meeting. Too often we are having the Before-Meeting in the car or on the elevator ride to see the client.

There are four elements that you want to be sure you have in place before the meeting.

1. **Background Information:** Who are you seeing? Why did they agree to meet? Who are the key players? What history do you have with them? What do they know about you? Where is the meeting? What do you have to share with them? Where is the client in the decision-making process?

    The salesperson needs to prepare you with all pertinent information. You have to be open and listen. Resist the temptation to make the salesperson feel that they have not prepared enough. You should be meeting well in advance of the client meeting and if more preparation is required, ask them to do it and meet later. Use this step to create partnership in your understanding and to build momentum for a productive call.

2. **Set Goal and Roles:** You need a specific and measurable goal for this call. Here are a few strong examples.

   - Have the client confirm that they need to take action on a key issue this year.

   - Learn about two problems the client is facing, verify that they have budget to spend on these issues and find out the approximate budget.

   - Gain agreement that the customer will share the internal research they have so you can review and provide your opinion.

   Once you have your goal, you can discuss roles. You need to agree to what role, you, as manager will play and how you will make it work. Often we say the salesperson will run the meeting and then, from the time we are greeted in reception, the client knows I am the manager and they want to deal with me. I chat with them as we walk to the meeting room. They sit proximate to me with the salesperson off to the side. That is not going to work! When you agree that the salesperson will run the meeting, discuss how that will be established from the start. Talk about how to sit in the meeting so the client is facing them. Plan how you will redirect to the salesperson when the client tries to direct conversation to you. Because you establish roles, do not assume that they will work — build a plan to make them work.

3. **Agree to Skill Development:** You are here to coach but why do it all after the meeting. Help set the salesperson up for success by coaching in advance. If you know they struggle with questioning, create a list of ten great questions in advance of the meeting with them. If you are worried that they have not presented this product before, do a quick demo of how you do it and then have them repeat it for you. Practice until you are 100% confident in their ability to do a great job. Want a gold medal opening — have them share theirs, critique and revise until perfect. Worried about pace or energy — give them tips and ideas to help them deliver what is needed to have an awesome meeting. If you are not sure what coaching they need, ask them what they would like help with. Once determined, don't wait for the meeting, coach now!

4. **Set Signs:** In our training sessions this is the point where participants think we have lost our minds. "You want me to have a signal that I use in the meeting?" Crazy as it seems, consider this — the meeting is bound to go differently than planned. The salesperson will do something that won't help or that you practiced how not to do. You will then have two choices — bite your tongue or jump in. But what if we add a third choice — have a sign that can help to coach in the moment with the goal of getting the meeting back on track — without intervention. Here are a few examples.

   • Salesperson talks too much — agree you will move your notepad towards them which means, stop talking and ask a question.

- Salesperson gets distracted and tends not to hear key points — same signal but it means, ask the client to give a little more detail on the last point.

- Salesperson rushes to solutions — signal means slow down and ask more questions.

- Salesperson talks really fast when they get nervous — signal is slow down.

- Salesperson is very nervous — they can signal you that they want you to jump in and help.

A NOT-SO-SECRET CODE

Years ago we had a junior salesperson who was new to Fusion Learning. She had an important meeting and we had fully prepared so that she was set up to do an excellent job. We had agreed that if she needed my help at any point during the meeting, she would place her pen on the table.

We walked into the meeting room with the clients and she was doing a nice job of engaging them in conversation prior to the start of the meeting. As we all settled into our seats, she placed her pen on the table. Odd, I thought, she seems to be in control and we practiced the start of the meeting, but, signal on, so I leaned forward and was about to start the meeting when she cleared her throat and delivered an excellent opening and picked up her pen.

She began to ask questions and the pen went down again. I leaned forward, about to jump in ... she asks a question and picks up her pen. No worries, let her run. Two minutes later, pen down, lean forward, she continues, picks up pen. You can imagine the rest.

I counted the times the pen went down and it was 28! She did great, I was a nervous wreck.

After the meeting, as we walked to the car, I casually mentioned our pen signal. She stopped, "Oh my goodness, did I put the pen down?"

"Only 28 times." She started to laugh and so did I.

The moral of the story, choose your signal carefully and be sure it is not something people do without thinking during a meeting.

A few tips for successful Before-Meeting preparation.

- Do it in advance (minimum one day) so that any additional work needed can be completed. Step one is often where you realize that more work must be done. If it is needed, stop the preparation meeting and ask the salesperson to do additional groundwork. Help them with what they need to do but allow them to do it. Ask them in future to come with that full level of preparation.

- The conversation should build confidence, not kill it. You are much more experienced than them (in most cases) and you could prepare to a greater level. If you expect them to be you, you will be disappointed and you will probably kill their confidence. Support them in doing what is needed so they learn how to be excellent at preparation.

- Coaching before is a lot better than tough feedback after. You know some of their weaknesses, help them with strategies and skills to overcome these difficulties before they are in front of the client. Practice, model, coach, suggest, review, write, do what it takes so they are ready for success, not ready for slaughter.

- Signals work. Just ask major league baseball. How amazing is it that you can coach them in the middle of a sales call and the client does not see it happening. (If you do not plan signals in advance and you resort to kicking under the table, they will notice.) Be careful, do not have multiple signs — one is great, two at the maximum.

- When setting roles, be realistic. If you will need to talk and share some expertise during the meeting, agree in advance. Set some talk-time guidance like 25-75 or 50-50 or 75-25. Be prepared to honor the agreement. You may feel like you need to break it and talk more but honoring your commitments is more important than a few minutes of talk time in one meeting.

During-the-Meeting

Let's be 100% honest — this is not a "normal" meeting. A normal meeting has one salesperson and the client(s). The salesperson is free to do as they please and are not looking over their shoulder. The client(s) is free to be open and share without concern for roles or dynamics in the meeting (at least not dynamics with the selling organization). Instead, there are multiple roles and multiple activities taking place.

- The sales manager is observing and taking notes to be able to provide feedback after the meeting.

- When the sales manager steps in, she is trying to sell and she must also be careful to be a model salesperson as she is being observed.

- The salesperson is selling and is fully aware that their every move is being monitored.

- The client(s) is aware of all that is happening and will also behave differently.

This is where it becomes very tempting to step in as captain of the play and run with it. You must resist taking on that role at all costs — unless you've set this up as part of the plan in the Before-Meeting preparation.

IN COGNITO

In working with a consumer packaged goods company a few years ago, I was in the field to observe their current sales behavior. I was traveling with a veteran salesperson who had been in her territory for many years. As we prepared to visit one grocery store she informed me that the store manager was very difficult and would never let her implement her ideas. "It's his store and he runs it. Salespeople are tolerated at best."

We enter the store and per the store policy we find the store manager to let him know we are in for a visit. She lets him know I am from head office and traveling with her today. We then survey the store and come up with two ideas to help sell her product. She reminds me that he will listen and will let her know he will consider them.

So, we find the manager and she lets him know there is extra stock in the back of an item currently on sale that could be put on an empty end display. Would he like us to move it? He smiles at her and replies, "Sure." I see she is taken aback by the agreement.

"Oh, okay. Ah, we will move it then."

"Thanks," he replies.

I see a small twinkle in her eye. "We also noticed that our stock in aisle four is a little out of alignment and only has four facings when it should have six. Okay if we fix it?"

"Please go ahead," he replies. And off we go to implement.

As we completed the two tasks, she was a bit stunned and confessed she couldn't figure out what just happened. Suddenly she stops and says, "Oh, I get it. There was a memo a few weeks back from his head office saying their buyers would be in the field visiting stores. He thinks you are from his head office." We both had a good chuckle and she asked if I could accompany her on all future visits to this store.

This story demonstrates the point above. It is not a normal meeting when salespeople are accompanied. Everybody acts differently, even the customer.

So how can we make a Field Coaching sales call as close to normal as possible. The roles we set out in preparation must be honored. The call can be one of three types.

1. **Manager Led (75-25):** This division of time should be used where the salesperson is new or not able to handle the specific meeting at hand. Be careful, manager led does not mean the salesperson is not involved. They can initiate the meeting, they can be the one to summarize at key points and they should lead the wrap-up.

2. **Dual Call (this is typically a 50-50 call):** Usually the salesperson will lead the opening and the investiga-

tion of needs. They will do their best to determine the priority needs of the client. They lead the inquiry portion of the call with minor help from the manager. When it comes time to begin solutions, they may require manager assistance and that is where the manager moves from coach/cheerleader to captain. Be careful not to elbow the salesperson out. Continue to have them engage. Plan in advance that when you move in that they're not to sit back but are to observe the client and ask questions to ensure the client is engaged in the solution.

3. **Salesperson Led (25-75):** This ratio is the toughest call for a manager. Why? The manager has the skills to do a better job in this meeting than the salesperson. At each point of the meeting, the manager has to remind themselves to allow the salesperson to work through it as opposed to being overcome by thoughts of "here is what they should be asking or saying." A simple analogy can help. When kids learn to ride a bike they start with training wheels. Parents are happy to observe and provide guidance from a distance. The sales call coaching equivalent is the preparation before the meeting. We are happy to observe and give guidance. Eventually the child will graduate and we will remove the training wheels. Parents get much more involved. No more distance, I am beside Johnny and, in fact, holding the handlebars. I do not want to let go. If I don't, Johnny will never learn. If I do, he will fall and get a bad scrape on his elbow when he falls. No big deal and, guess what, he no longer wants to fall and the fear of falling will force

him to ride. Same on the sales call. If I hold the handlebars (me talking), my salesperson will never learn to sell. If I let go, they will falter (fall) but it will be a minor scrape and I will be there to apply the bandage (after-call coaching). Let them learn by allowing them to do things differently than you might and to make a few mistakes. When the child learns to ride and the parent no longer stresses when they want to use the bike, the parent's life and stress level are much easier. Same for you — let them learn and your life as a manager will be easier.

Let's take a look at when we need to intervene in a sales call. There are definitely times when it might not be a minor scrape and intervention is required. We don't usually have a signal for "you are giving incorrect information." No worries, gently interject and, most importantly, turn it back to the salesperson at the earliest opportunity. Too often, I see managers jump in and, once in, they stay. Take the 20-second timeout by jumping into the meeting but then return to coach position by giving "the ball" back to the salesperson.

In observing during a sales meeting, look for a great coaching moment — that moment when you felt you needed to jump in but you chose not to and then a few minutes later exactly what you intended to do is done by the salesperson. Pause on that moment as they just built their confidence — they did something really well and you will be giving them positive feedback after the call. You also built your confidence in them as they went where you felt they needed to go with no prompting from you. Imagine the consequences if you had jumped in ...

After-the-Meeting Feedback

Coaching at this stage in the process is probably the most comfortable. However, employ the four-step Effective Feedback skills from Chapter Three — no sandwiches or seagulls here.

It is important to note that there are really two parts to the debrief — feedback and review of the sales call/next steps. Please, please separate these two conversations. One builds confidence/skill (feedback) and one builds an action plan. If we mix the two, the feedback will be lost.

Start with feedback. Here's a quick refresher on Effective Feedback.

1. What do you feel went well in the preparation and execution of that sales meeting? Get them to start with the positive. Stop them from going negative. Don't allow them to laundry list eight things that went well. Draw their focus to two or three strengths from their preparation and the meeting. Get them to give specifics to support the strengths. Pause to celebrate success.

2. Here is what I saw you do well. Don't just agree to their list. Add to it. Be specific and genuine. There are always positives even on a poor call. Reinforce what they must continue to do and build confidence.

3. What will you do differently next time? Work on skills. Be careful of them pointing out what the customer could do differently. If they suggest a change, ask how and why they will do differently next time.

4. Here are my suggestions. Do not give a long list. Give one or two suggestions and discuss them. Do they

agree? How will they implement these ideas? What benefit do they see to implementing them?

Once the feedback conversation is complete, move to a review of the call and what action steps they need to take to win the business.

Feedback builds confidence and skill; action plans make sure that we maximize the outcome from the meeting.

Frequency of Coaching

As I mentioned at the start of the chapter, few organizations are doing enough Field Coaching. Why? It is not an organizational priority. It is expected that salespeople will have managers travel with them and it does happen. It usually happens on important deals rather than as a regular coaching activity.

The big win for sales teams is that those who practice frequent Field Coaching are constantly improving the skills of their sales team. They see exactly what is happening on the field and they coach any struggles their sales team is facing. If you are questioning some of your results, take the time to view every salesperson in action and help each to create an action plan for improvement. Track and watch how your results improve with the improvements in the team.

I believe some of the infrequency of Field Coaching relates to the fact that "Field Coaching" is only practiced at the front line. Managers are not observing managers coaching and managers do what they see their managers doing not what they are saying so it becomes a D priority — "I'll do it if nothing else needs doing."

Managers Field Coach Managers

Good to great organizations implement Field Coaching across the organization. They do not feel that salespeople need Field Coaching; they feel that everyone in the (sales) organization needs Field Coaching. Here are some examples.

- **Team Meetings:** Your manager meets with you before a team meeting to review your preparation and to help make sure it will be a solid 8-out-of-10 meeting. She then sits in and observes (with maybe a 5-minute Q&A for the team or a small piece on the agenda). After the meeting you follow the feedback model to build your confidence and skill in team meetings.

- **One-on-Ones:** On this one, you might skip the Before–Meeting. Why? Because if they know you are attending, they will do maximum preparation and do their best One-on-One ever. You want to see the standard One-on-One. Look at their calendar and show up at the start of a meeting and ask to sit in. See it exactly as they planned. After you have a feedback discussion. If preparation is an area for improvement then schedule to sit in on another One-on-One and for that one meet with them in advance to help them prepare.

- **Tough Conversation Coaching:** Sales managers often need to have tough conversations with salespeople. Help them prepare and even practice for the meeting. Sit in and view or allow them to conduct on their own. Either way, meet after for feedback.

- **Coaching on Field Coaching:** The sales leader accompanies the sales manager who is providing Field Coaching for the salesperson. The sales leader observes the meeting before the call and observes the feedback after the call. It is difficult for them to attend the meeting as three may be too many but they will see the majority of the coaching. After the feedback session with the salesperson, they meet with the sales manager only and they conduct a feedback conversation following our four steps.

I CAN'T BELIEVE IT'S THE COACHING

A few years ago we worked with a contact center leader to help improve the skills of his representatives and the skills of his supervisors and managers. He had 3 managers, 18 supervisors and about 220 representatives on the phone. They did an excellent job at changing how people were coached and managed. They implemented our system for One-on-Ones and for Field (observation) Coaching. The leader was pleased with early results but wanted to make sure great coaching was happening.

He sat in on One-on-Ones his three managers had with their supervisors and coached them to be even more successful. They sat in on supervisors' One-on-Ones and coached them. One day he called and said he was thinking of going to the next level and personally sitting in on all 18 supervisors' One-on-Ones to reinforce what his managers had coached on and to show how important coaching was in their organization. We encouraged him, provided he had the managers' support. He did and he provided great coaching and a great message about coaching.

The net results? His business improved by 20% across the board. It improved so much that when he saw the numbers one month, he had his analysts check all of their work as he felt they could not have delivered such a big improvement. No mistakes had been made. They had dramatically improved the business. Coaching works!

Field Coaching needs to be an organizational activity, not an activity for sales managers alone. It should be scheduled and the standard should be maintained across the organization. All members of the team should be observed regardless of tenure, experience or level in the organization. Field Coaching will lead to increased engagement as it helps us all to improve and to win.

To be the captain and score the deal is the point of all this effort, of course, but the coaching and cheerleading are also part of the training and must be practiced — on and off the field. Feedback should improve confidence and skill. Recording the score and dealing with the stats will take place — it's called the Performance Review.

Performance Reviews Should Not Be About the Boxes

THE RESEARCH

The Question 2013: "Sales Representatives receive annual written performance reviews."

The Response: 88% of leaders said yes.

The Question: "Our written performance reviews add value and help to cause positive change in our people."

The Response: 6.7 out of 10, with 30% being 8 out of 10 or better and 40% being a 6 out of 10 or lower.

STRENGTHS

- Performance reviews are being done, annually in many organizations.
- Reviews are closely linked to compensation.

OPPORTUNITY

- In a lot of cases the format is highly structured and both parties spend time trying to "fit" feedback into the form.
- Provide lots of clear, specific, positive feedback.
- Create an action plan for what needs to be done differently.

DEFINITION

- Performance reviews should be in a simple format and loaded with feedback — lots on what is going well and lots on areas for improvement. The feedback must come from multiple constituents (managers, colleagues, direct reports, suppliers, customers, contractors, etc.). An action plan must be created, implemented and monitored.

FUSION LEARNING POINT OF VIEW

- The five-step process collects feedback from various reviewers, provides a document for review and includes two meetings with the salesperson.

GOAL

There is so much data that you may need to wait 18 to 24 months before repeating the process. It will be 4 hours of the manager's time that will lead to improved performance.

How much value is created by the reviews being done in your organization?

The first time I received a performance review that follows the process I will outline was in 1997. It was by far the best review I had ever received. I still have it.

At the time I worked for a training and consulting organization based in Boston and I was located in Toronto. My boss was located in New York. The review was 7 pages of commentary that had input from 14 people, including direct reports in Toronto and Chicago, professionals in our offices around the globe, senior executives of the firm and customers. I was delighted with some of the positive comments that helped me to really see the value I created in our firm. The opportunities for improvement had some strong ideas for me and they were needed. I was vaguely aware of some of my opportunities but the review helped to move them from fuzzy to specific.

Performance Review System

As noted earlier many review systems follow a rigid structure that forces managers to apply to all employees — not very engaging at all. Our system is much more free-flow and interactive, but that does not mean there is not a great deal of time spent on the process and that there is no structure. In fact, our system has five steps (and sub-steps within each).

1. Agree with Performer to a List of Reviewers
2. Collect Feedback
3. Create a Feedback Document
4. Feedback Meeting #1 — present and discuss

5. Feedback Meeting #2 — finalize review and agree on action plan

The timing for the five steps for you as manager from start to finish is 4 hours. Step one is 15 minutes. Step two is 15 minutes. Step three will take 1.5 hours. Steps four and five are 1 hour each. This timing may be slightly longer than it would take to fill in a review but the hope is that this review is so comprehensive that it is not needed annually (I do mine for direct reports every 18 to 24 months).

1. Agree with Performer to a List of Reviewers

This step is very important. You must get a list that will give great representation of different relationships and different viewpoints. I always ask who they would like on the list and I almost always edit the list. The key questions to think about will help you create a comprehensive and far-reaching list.

- Diversity in levels and roles
- Strong relationships and tougher relationships represented
- Enough interaction to comment (be careful on this because those with not much interaction will throw in comments that may not have facts and data to back them up)
- Experience in providing specific feedback

The goal is about 12 to 15 people to provide feedback and to get 100% submission from them — if this is the list of people you want to provide feedback then you need them to comment (more on this in step 2).

2. Collect Feedback

Your goal is 100% response so you need to ask nicely, remind gently and ultimately push for a response. The 100% is important so you do not get bias — you agreed to the list so be sure you have plenty of feedback, from a variety of sources. Once in a while someone will say that they have not had enough interaction to comment, in which case it is fine to remove them from the list.

The initial request for feedback should look something like the following:

Hello everyone,

I am asking for your feedback as part of Sarah's performance review.

You know how valuable it is towards your growth and self-awareness when you receive feedback. Now it's time to give that same privilege to one of your team.

Please respond to me confidentially with a thoughtful list of:

- Green Flags (What she is doing well)
- Red Flags (Where you would like her to improve in the future)
- Any overall comments or additional information that you feel would be beneficial in the review process

Please be detailed and specific. All comments will be grouped and not attributed to an individual.

I would appreciate your response by Tuesday, October 23, with a goal of 100% response.
Cheers, Kevin

Give about 2 weeks from the time of sending your note to the feedback deadline. After 1 week, send the first reminder, being careful to delete those who have already responded. The reminder should be a forward of the original message with a brief reminder note.

I typically find about 25% response rate on original message. After the reminder and a few days before deadline, it jumps to about 75%. On the morning of the final day, my third message goes to those who have not responded — and I often give them another day to get their feedback in.

With this final reminder, I usually get everyone. If I am missing one and they are important, I will then reach out to them personally or by phone. There are times when I miss one or two but most often I can get 100% by being pleasantly persistent.

During the feedback collection stage, be sure to write your feedback on the person and submit it. You do not want the feedback collected to bias what you have to say. Your input will also help you to see where you are in line with others and where you may differ or have blind spots for your employee.

As the responses come in, I have a folder in my e-mail where I collect the feedback and also keep my reminders — everything neatly organized in one place. Be careful to know who has responded and who has not — the reminders lose face if you remind someone who has submitted. Once you have completed the review, send a brief thank you to all who participated so they know the review is complete and their feedback has been delivered.

3. Create Feedback Document

This step takes about 90 minutes — be sure to block the time and complete the review in one sitting as this will allow you to maximize your understanding of the feedback. Here are the sub-steps to creating the performance review that I employ.

- Read each person's feedback in full. This step allows you to understand the comments from everyone in context. It will allow you to sort the feedback easily.

- Now it is time to pull the feedback out of the individual e-mails/documents into one Word file. Pull all positive feedback (Green Flags) and put at the beginning of the document. Pull all opportunities for improvement (Red Flags) and place them at the end of the document. You are left with overall comments and these can go in an overview section at the very beginning of the review or they can be added to the Green or Red Flag sections, as appropriate. (Practical Tip: there are a lot of comments so I tend to cut and paste versus copy — a lot easier to not get lost in what has been moved. Also leave the styles alone and format the document once at the end.)

- You now have one document with all comments. Typically with 12 to 15 reviewers this document will be 5 to 8 pages long. For more junior positions it will be shorter. Print and read the document in full and, as you do, start to create a list of categories for the feedback. You can use your company Values, a job description or a competency model to help connect the feedback to your organization. You want four to six categories for the positive feedback and three to four categories for the areas of improvement plus overall comments. Overall comments are ones that the reviewers identified as overall or ones that you feel are a great positive commentary on overall performance.

- Once you have the categories, go through the printed list and assign a category code for each comment. As an example, I use our five Fusion Learning Values as part of my category codes:

  C — Communicate and Collaborate

  D — Deliver Excellence

  G — Learn and Grow

  L — Lead Creatively

  A — Celebrate and Appreciate

  Then apply this organizing step to the comments and document.

  You may find after coding that you only have one or two comments for a category. I usually move them to another spot where they fit, although if they are critical comments and I want them to really stand out, I will leave them as a category.

  You will also find some comments that do not "fit" with the organizational models you use to help. Pay attention for these and do not spread them out to fit your model — they may need their own category. As an example, a few years ago I had someone who struggled with responsiveness. When I first did their review these comments were spread out in Deliver Excellence, Communicate and Collaborate and Lead Creatively based on the specific emphasis. The responsiveness message was being diluted among other feedback. When I created a responsiveness category, I was able to put four comments in it and it was very helpful in making the number one item on their action plan — improve responsiveness.

- Print the document and reread to see that you have categorized correctly. If a comment seems out of place, move it to another category where it fits better.

    Caution: It is at this point that you may need to slightly alter comments so that you protect anonymity. The goal is to give exact wording of the feedback but you must also be sure it does not identify who provided the information — especially on the opportunities for improvement. Use your judgment as to whether it is necessary to protect anonymity or go to the provider of the feedback and ask them if they approve of you providing the comment verbatim.

- And finally make the document pretty — format it (see Sample Performance Review at the end of this chapter).

4. Feedback Meeting #1 — Present and Discuss

You have put a lot of hard work into creating the document, now it is time for the first meeting to review the feedback with your team member.

Caution: Do not give the review to the team member in advance. In a five-to-seven-page review there is a lot of commentary and a lot that they can react to. It is very helpful and prudent to be there with them. Let me illustrate with a story.

LOST IN THE PRESENTATION

I had prepared a very detailed review for a team member. We had our review scheduled for 11 am. When the time came I had a small issue that I needed to deal with so I gave them the review and asked them to read it in their office while I took care of the issue. Fifteen minutes later we met and I could tell right away that they were upset.

When I asked why, they immediately started referring to all of the opportunities for improvement and how they were tough and they started to get very defensive about the Red Flags. When asked about the Green Flags, the conversation almost immediately went back to the Red Flags. It then hit me and I asked them, "What did you read first?"

"My opportunities for improvement," was the answer.

"Did you read the positive comments?"

"Yes, but they did not really effect me."

"Was it hard to read them because you were upset about the opportunities?"

"Yes."

I had passed out the review and they had read the review in the exact way we say you should never deliver feedback — they started with the negatives. Shame on me for letting the hard work of this review get lost in translation. My mistake and why I am always present when they read the review. I have also adjusted my process so that we separate strengths from opportunities just as we do in providing Effective Feedback.

When it is time for the performance review meeting, I lay out the process.

1. Both of us will read in detail the overall comments and the strengths.

2. We will discuss your overall views on the strengths.

3. We will agree to three key themes in strengths that most resonate with you.

4. We will discuss the strengths in detail.

5. Both of us will read in detail the opportunities for improvement.

6. We will discuss your overall views on the opportunities.

7. We will agree to three key themes in opportunities that most resonate with you.

8. We will discuss the opportunities in detail.

9. We will begin to think about an action plan with you having a take away to come back to me at the second review meeting with a detailed action plan.

As they read it so do I. When they have finished reading a section, we begin our discussion. The question flow tends to follow this pattern.

- Please give me your overall reaction to the strengths outlined in the review.

- Is the view reflective of your overall strengths? That is, do you see it as being truthful to your performance?

- What are three or four key messages you get from the strengths section of the review (may need to allow time for quick reread of the section)? Be sure to note these comments so you have a clear view of how they are seeing their strengths.

- Let's look at a couple of comments you are particularly proud of. Which ones stand out to you?

- Please give me your overall reaction to the opportunities outlined in the review.

- Is the view reflective of your overall opportunities? That is, do you see it as being truthful to your performance?

- What are three or four key messages you get from the opportunities section of the review (may need to allow time for quick reread of the section)? Be sure to note these comments so you have a clear view of how they are seeing their opportunities.

- Looking at category "X" (pick the one that is most prominent in needing improvement), do you feel you need to improve and, if so, why? What are some ideas you have on how to improve?

- I may repeat for a second improvement category if I want an action plan to take on two opportunities or I may ask that the action plan only tackle one area at the beginning.

Once we have conducted our discussion and they are feeling comfortable with the review, we discuss how and when they will create the action plan. Some only need a few days, while others may need a week or so. Schedule the follow-up meeting now and be sure they own creating the action plan.

A few cautions for this meeting.

- When reading the comments, both positive and opportunities, you may hear comments like, "I know who said that" or "That came from Joe." Be sure to caution them that the feedback has been disguised where necessary and also caution them that when they try to guess they will often be wrong. (This is not a lie. When I have heard people say "This came from Joe," they are often wrong.)

- The saying "The truth hurts," can often be true. You have collected a lot of feedback and the truth will be there. Some people will become emotional when they see in print what they know is an area of weakness. You must take time and allow them to process the review with you. Do not allow them to leave in an emotional state.

- You may get push back on some areas of opportunity. Think about this prior to the meeting and be prepared to hold a detailed discussion. Here are some of the questions that I find work where they are rejecting the data.

  — Is there some degree of truth in these comments? If yes, what is true?

  — Explain why you feel there are "X" (a number) comments on this opportunity that seem to support it being important.

— The opportunity is "X." Give me an example of when you did this well. Give me an example of where you did this poorly.

— Have you ever received feedback on this opportunity in the past? Please tell me about that.

Be sure to end the meeting on a positive view. I sometimes give the holiday gift analogy.

Feedback is like a gift. It is all beautifully wrapped and when you first see it from a distance it looks all shiny and pretty. You are excited as you tear back the packaging and then it is open ... and it is not so pretty and not to your liking ... but you must smile and act excited and express a heartfelt thank-you. Yet inside, you are no longer rejoicing.

Let your team member know that it will take time to process the feedback. Encourage them to set the review aside for 24 hours and then to reread it. Encourage them to spend a lot of time on the positives and not to get lost in the opportunities. Check in with them at about the 48-hour mark to make sure they are processing well. If they are hung up on the opportunities, be sure to sit down with them and review the positives. Do not allow them to live in negativity.

5. Feedback Meeting #2 — Finalize Review and Agree on an Action Plan

Time to move from review to action. Lots of hard work by you, the reviewee and the reviewers — be sure to get strong ROTI (return on time invested) by agreeing to a solid action plan.

The first step in the meeting is to revisit the review. Are there any questions? What is their feeling after having it for some time? In the odd case, I have been asked if I would remove a comment that they feel is strong or touches a nerve. I don't like to do this but as long as they are committed to change in their action plan, this can be a way to gain further buy-in.

Review their action plan and help them to move it from good to great (see Figure 9). Be sure it is a SMART action plan — Specific, Measurable, Attainable, Realistic and Timely. Ask them how you can help. Gain their commitment that they want to improve and that they see value for them personally in improving. Remind them you are looking for progress, not perfection. Set a plan for how you will review their progress on the action plan in your monthly One-on-Ones.

Performance Reviews should not be cookie cutter and should not be viewed with dread by the sales manager (the reviewer) or the salesperson (the reviewee). They should be thoughtful, provide a chance to look at overall performance from many perspectives, add value and improve engagement.

The ultimate outcome will be an Action Plan that will lead to productive One-on-Ones, winning coaching and motivated salespeople who can be celebrated and rewarded. The definitive upshot will be a highly engaged team and a great sales culture!

SALESPERSON PERFORMANCE REVIEW ACTION PLAN

Increase my leadership and contributory profile during sales team meetings by:

- Contributing more ideas and information leveraging my experience

- Demonstrating support for Fusion process and practices where applicable

- Take formal responsibility for sales team leadership in VP's absence

Be more mindful of the contribution other staff make to my sales success and that of the rest of the sales team and provide more recognition to all more frequently and consistently:

- Send a hand written thank you card for any design support provided on won deals

- Take a team member out to lunch who has been working hard on one of my projects

Further increase my coaching and guidance of sales team members, both formally and informally:

- Check in on a regular basis with those team members who I don't formally coach to provide offers of support and guidance

- Ensure I maintain the rigor to the formal coaching process I have established with the two team members assigned to me

Place emphasis on expanding my focus beyond financial services clients to create more breadth and diversity in my accounts:

- Ensure my Top 20 and Farm Club Lists have a variety of business verticals and industries to be focused on

- Revisit and update my Key Account Plans to add an account plan for a company outside financial services and insurance

© 2014 Fusion Learning Inc.

SAMPLE PERFORMANCE REVIEW

Overall Comments

The Fusion Learning team is unanimous in applauding your success in your first year.

- I am thrilled with her: 9+ out of 10. Her personality, smarts and effort make Fusion a much better and richer firm.

- She is overachieving in my eyes in her two key areas of responsibility.

- Fusion is very fortunate to have a leader with the special characteristics that she brings to the table.

- I sometimes forget that she hasn't been at Fusion for ages; she has become such an integral part of the team. I really value her contribution, leadership and am learning a lot from her.

- She's made a lot of progress at Fusion and in the sales training industry in a very short period of time — she's a fast learner.

- Being a leader at Fusion is a challenging role — and she keeps things in perspective and is cool under pressure.

- She is like an older sister and a pleasure to work with. I believe she is a huge asset to the Fusion team and the place just wouldn't be the same without her. I am very happy and fortunate to work closely with her.

- Overall, she is great to work with. She is collaborative and open to ideas and generally proactive.

Strengths

Deliver Excellence

- At least during the times that I have been involved in "enablement" calls she has been very thorough and well prepared.

- She is client focused.

- Her strength is in her communication skills. Her follow-through is very good and also her attention to detail.

- Wonderfully process minded.

- Is making her way up the ladder in receiving Fusion revenue and her target for the year.

- Takes initiative; loves to learn new things and noticed her skills increase in areas outside of her expertise.

- Knows how to tackle a project/task by processing it appropriately in her head and is not afraid to ask questions (takes initiative to understand things).

- Great with process and attention to detail.

- Responsive (when I've needed to get in touch with her regarding specific accounts, she has been very quick to respond). Example: I was at a client's office in Montreal last January. Some materials were missing and I couldn't get in touch with the project manager. She quickly handled the issue and faxed the documents that I required to the hotel.

- Individual sales performance is strong.

- Thorough. Example: When she involves me in a project, she provides me with access to all the information

I require and follows up and gives feedback at the end of a session.

- Intelligent.
- Customer and project accountability.
- Methodical problem solving.
- Process oriented. She is on revenue recognition — a tough gig — but she is making consistent small improvements.
- Well organized — strong process orientation.

Lead Creatively

- Fusion has experienced great sales growth and she must be credited with having a positive leadership impact.
- She is an excellent leader and coach, both to the sales and backstage team. She takes the time to understand your issue and coach you to find the answer versus telling you what to do.
- She has a very methodical/process oriented way of thinking. This inspires confidence, particularly when we're dealing with yellow/red flag issues because she never panics.
- She is very helpful, but more than that, when she helps you, she does so 110%. A personal example is tips for my running or camping, and I know that she is helping Joe after hours with his finance homework. Classy!
- Great sense of humor, fun to work with and ability to lighten up when needed.
- Good coach, mentor and even a confidante.

- Innovative and fresh ideas around driving skills drills and prospecting.

- Her sense of humor is amazing (and appropriate!).

- Great leader.

- Jovial when not engaged in work.

- I think she is able to earn trust quickly, and delivers on her promises. She often takes the time to teach her organizational techniques to others, and that has helped me personally. I would like to see that continue.

- Humor. She has a great sense of humor which has a fine impact on our culture.

- Initiative. She is taking more and more as far as e-mail ideas (i.e., sending a note about PowerPoint template), standing up in biz review meeting the other day to draw a diagram on the flipchart and compare our biz with making widgets — in a fun and learning driven way.

- Makes an effort with people (with me anyways).

- On top of Sales processes — Meetings, salesforce.com, Forecast, Revenue recognition, etc.

- Sense of humor.

- Total team player.

- It sounds like she dealt quickly with Mark — that is *very* good. Organizations, as you know, often are quick to hire and slow to fire.

- Acts very professional when time calls for it, but has a great sense of humor (on-site and off-site) as well.

- Has stepped up to her role very quickly.

Learn & Grow

- She has quickly adapted to the "Fusion Way" of doing things.

- The process she uses for conducting meetings absolutely follows the format advocated in the Fusion sales training.

- She demonstrates the sales skills we teach.

- Great at modeling and reinforcing of Fusion models.

- Sales meetings are consistently an 8 out of 10.

- Represents Fusion well.

- Seems to be very involved with her clients. Example: Took time out of her schedule to come and watch me deliver a half-day session for a client in Toronto. Led an excellent feedback discussion with me after the training that gave me positive reinforcement and areas to focus on for future deliveries.

- Sales meetings follow the process/standards we teach, reinforcing that our stuff "works!"

Communicate and Collaborate

- Good listener.

- Very open to new ideas/processes. Even if she does have some reservations, she'll really try it out and see how the idea/process works.

- Willing to find a solution.

- Easy to approach — open and willing to help.

- Great at encouraging/coaching the use of Fusion communication skills (i.e., I had a tough client situation and she coached me on our handling objections model).
- Is a great tutor and easy to understand/learn from.
- Excellent communicator.

Values Driven

- Her personal values appear to be aligned to Fusion's and she seems to be a good fit.
- Honest.
- Genuine, "real" and present.
- Consistent positive attitude (respectful to everyone at Fusion).
- Very professional. She is easy to work with and is always extremely professional.

Opportunities

Deliver Excellence

- Extend some more help/support on joint calls with Sales team.
- Work more closely with Derrick to ramp him up faster (i.e., review his account list and remove accounts he shouldn't waste his time on, etc.) — more "hands on" and directive at this stage.
- Build stronger relationships with the Fusion Player network — get to know us and help us get to know her.

- More of a proactive approach to Fusion offerings and solutions.

- More occasional check-ins to see how things are going — asking if there's any help/support needed with any sales opportunities.

- Question/confirm skills should be used to listen/understand versus getting to your response (at times can be condescending).

- My own experience is that she does not connect a lot with me, particularly when it comes to follow-up, for example:
  - No unprompted update on leads provided (sales or offer to help ID prospects for Sales role).
  - No unprompted reconnect on potential client engagements that have been discussed.
  - No reaching out to see what support I can provide for sales efforts.

- Use Fusion Players to help drive sales efforts (invite us to a sales meeting once in a while).

- More clearly state what she wants or what her expectations are.

- I spend a lot of time with Sam and Kerri and they keep me informed and involved — this is not the case with her.

Approachability

- During moments of stress or when she's in a bad mood, she becomes short with you, impatient and even condescending at times. I find she'll throw your words back at you in a way that makes what you said sound ridiculous. This rattles my confidence and distracts me from the issue at hand. I think she can work on her approachability during these situations.

- Softer touch with others, to avoid seeming aloof.
- When busy can be unapproachable at times.
- When in the midst of processes can miss the "heart/human" element at times.
- Her interactions with people could do more around "engage the heart," as we teach in our programs.
- Not always the most approachable person in the office if busy — perhaps door closed/head down time would help with interruptions.
- Sometimes feels like she is not listening when trying to engage her attention (talking to her) as she takes some time to react and respond (even though she may be in the middle of something, she could possibly say something like "one second" or "be right with you" so you know she is listening).

Lead Creatively

- It's critical that Derrick succeeds — invest the time and energy up front to increase his likelihood of success.
- Keep the solid base of sales meetings — and perhaps mix it up a bit — push the creative side a bit more.
- Collaborate on an integrated Marketing/Sales approach to fill Fusion opportunity pipeline.

- Dedicate more focus on creating a sales strategy to drive Strategic Blue*PRINT* (i.e., solution focus, sector focus, targeted account focus, etc.).

- More integrated approach to prospecting and marketing. It is a leading indicator for our strategy and important and I don't feel that there is strong collaboration.

- More proactive and consistent use of Confirm skill in sales meetings.

- I was not told about the departure of Mark and I don't know much at all about the new sales rep.

- I have a folder in Outlook that captures all non-client specific e-mails from Fusion staff — I have never opened a file for her because I have never received any mail that is non-client specific.

- Keeping up with the consistency of One-on-Ones, and paying attention to the progression versus repetition.

- Networking and investing more time with the team to share "intell" on named accounts/contacts/6-degrees of separation — I believe there's a lot more we can do to leverage tacit knowledge of the team.

Learn & Grow

- Better understanding of Learning Profession, resources and offerings.

- Better understanding of key clients in named accounts.

- How much observation has she done of our programs? Should she do that every quarter or something to stay connected?

- I was a little disappointed that some of the strategic elements from the off-site do not seem to be showing up in her "all important" department.

- Keep players current on pipeline activities — we have contacts and networks that might be helpful.

- Make more attempts to use our own Sales Toolkit internally, so that we can speak from personal experience. These tools work! And they work for us.

- Be proactive in how she would like to prepare for and use advisory board meetings — that's where strategy, especially sales strategy, should be front and center and it should come first from her.

Attitude + Skills + Disciplines = Engagement

Thank you for reading *Engage Me*! You might be thinking, now what? As mentioned at the beginning of this book, aim for progress not perfection. Please do not attempt to make wholesale change. In implementing, I would suggest you follow, in order, the three sections.

Start with Attitude and make sure you have the foundation of a great sales culture. You will need the skills and the management disciplines to fully realize the culture and *you* need to start with a positive attitude in *you* and in the sales organization. Make some culture changes — try to start two or three new things, try to stop two or three things that are not productive and try to continue the things that are working.

In working with hundreds of organizations on culture, one question is asked often, "Is change possible?" My answer is always the same. "Absolutely, and it will take hard work." We stopped our beer Fridays at Fusion at one point and our culture felt it. People started to talk about the good old days and the things we used to do. We restarted them and the fun factor went back up. Yes, this was not the only factor but I can say that our culture did dip a few years ago and we have more than recovered. Change is possible.

When you have made a few cultural adjustments, move to Skill changes.

You have the skills you need to be a great coach. Are you using them with conscious choice? Question Better, Confirm More and Respond Less need 3 months of solid practice to change habits. Be sure to share with others the changes you are attempting to make and engage them in supporting you. Track the successful conversations where you employed Thoughtful Questions and allowed salespeople to solve their own issues. How much time have you saved? How much more have they bought in? What sales targets are achieved that may have been missed? Celebrate your wins and learn from opportunities missed.

As you become comfortable with some changes in the skills, add the four steps to Effective Feedback. Watch out for the sandwich and create feedback dialogues rather than giving feedback. The attitude or sales culture plus coaching skills and Effective Feedback are the foundations — the fundamentals. These changes will lead to changes in engagement *and* in results.

With those in place, begin to change your sales management Disciplines, one at a time.

Start with the low-hanging fruit, which could most benefit from some changes. Start with sales meetings as they are simpler to change and you can see immediate impact. Follow the six keys to success and you will get it!

One-on-Ones will take more effort to change. Reread Chapter Five and get very clear in your mind which structure you will use. Create a form, or copy ours, but make sure you are clear and committed to change. The degree of difficulty with this skill is higher. Your first One-on-One in a different format will take a long time (you are not sure of what you are doing, nor are they). Let your people know you are making a change, share the process and ask for their help. Get their feedback. My experience is that by the third One-on-One you will have a good flow and you will be having dramatically different conversations.

Pipeline management and reviews are a more *tactical* change. You could start with this discipline before One-on-Ones or after. Share the pipeline types with your sales team and let them know they are accountable to always be in touch with the shape of their pipeline. They own it and they need to manage it. Use weekly or bi-weekly conversations to hold the mirror up to them so they can be honest about the shape of their pipeline. Most importantly, if it is not Healthy, be sure they have a plan to get it there in a reasonable amount of time.

Changing your sales culture and your sales management disciplines will work significantly better if it is a team effort. Fusion Learning would be excited to help so please reach out to us at www.fusionlearninginc.com. Everything in *Engage Me* is practiced in our office. Please call if you would like to come for a tour and see the discipline in action.

My very best wishes for success in creating a world-class sales culture with engaged sales team members who consistently deliver over-plan performance.

Resources to Help You — Engage Me

Now that you've finished reading *Engage Me*, you are faced with the opportunity to put some of the ideas and models into practice with your people. To help you make real and sustainable change within your organization, I strongly encourage you to take advantage of the sales effectiveness resources below.

At Fusion, we help sales leaders and salespeople perform better. As one of the top 10 sales training firms in North America, we offer practical customized sales training programs to drive the right kind of sales behaviors. Our clients realize dramatic and sustainable increases in sales productivity, meeting activity, sales win rates and client experience ratings.

A full range of resources for improving your sales organization are available at www.fusionlearninginc.com, including videos, articles and Fusion's blog. Details on how Fusion Learning can increase your sales opportunities, shorten your sales cycle, and close more profitable business are also here.

Published Articles

Whether it's an emerging trend, results of recent research or a client case study, the latest perspectives from Fusion Learning provide insights on a variety of sales effectiveness

topics. Visit us at: www.fusionlearninginc.com/resource_
library/overview.

Video Gallery

We have over 75 short videos highlighting specific topics
that are shaping sales today, featuring senior Fusion leaders
and sales executives. www.fusionlearninginc.com/resource_
library/overview.

Executive Breakfast Series

Fusion Learning hosts an executive breakfast series for
sales executives and HR leaders. In dynamic presentations
and conversations, leaders reveal insights, opinions and
unexpected answers to the challenges facing sales organizations today. Short video and audio clips are available at:
www.fusionlearninginc.com/resource_library/executive-
breakfast-series.

About Fusion Learning

Being a significant contributor to the growth and success of North America's leading sales organizations has helped to propel Fusion Learning from "start-up" in 2000 to one of the industry's fastest growing and most successful sales effectiveness firms today.

With a blue chip client list that includes companies as diverse as 3M, American Express, BMO, Molson Coors, Pfizer, PwC, SAS, Scotiabank and BlackRock, Fusion specializes in customizing programs that are culturally specific to your business.

Our integrated curriculum addresses key insights from our research, including:

- Programs for Sales Executives: Strategic Sales Blue-PRINT, Sales Leader BluePRINT, StorySelling, Sales Culture Diagnostic.

- Programs for Sales Managers: Sales Leader BluePRINT, Managing Activity & Results, Sales Coaching, Leading & Motivating, Conducting World Class One-on-Ones, Facilitating Engaging Sales Meetings, StorySelling.

- Programs for Salespeople: Consultative Selling, Winning Negotiations, Strategic Account Management, StorySelling, Proactive Prospecting, SmartSelling, Customer Service Excellence, Individual Sales Blue-PRINT, Influential Presentations.

Recognized for Sales Training Excellence

Fusion Learning has been named by *Selling Power* magazine as one of the Top 10 Sales Training firms in North America for the second consecutive year.

The Top 10 Sales Training Companies list recognizes firms that excel in helping sales managers improve the performance of their sales teams. Firms on the list need to demonstrate:

- a proven track record of delivering results for sales leaders and sales teams,
- innovative methods to both deliver and reinforce training,
- customizable solutions and training methods to ensure high-quality results and
- offerings that have been customized for the evolving needs of today's sales organizations.

For more information, visit www.fusionlearninginc.com or call us today at (416) 424-2999.

Sales Culture Trends 2013

Fusion Learning's Sales Culture Survey, conducted in 2006, 2010 and 2013, is quoted at the start of each chapter of *Engage Me*. We included the data for you to use as a reference point for your organization.

As a Sales leader, understanding how your organization stacks up against others is critically important. Fusion has conducted comprehensive research with leading sales organizations and collected, tabulated and interpreted the data.

For a free copy of "Sales Culture Trends 2013," visit www.fusionlearninginc.com/programs/sales-culture-diagnostic, or call us today at (416) 424-2999. We ask only one thing of you – share the information and insights with other leaders in your organization.

Sales Culture Diagnostic

Until now, taking a comprehensive measure of your sales force has been expensive and time consuming. Now, you can use our Sales Culture Diagnostic to benchmark your sales organization. For more information on how this efficient and effective tool and other resources can get your sales organization to world class, visit www.fusionlearninginc.com or call us today at (416) 424-2999.